Ian Sansom is a novelist, journalist and broadcaster. He is the author of more than a dozen books, including *The Truth About Babies: An A-Z, Paper: An Elegy, September 1, 1939: A Biography of a Poem*, and the Mobile Library and the County Guides series of novels. He writes for the *Guardian*, the *Times Literary Supplement*, the *Spectator* and the *Irish Times*. He is a regular presenter on BBC Radio 3 and Radio 4. In this volume, he brings together decades of his notes on the various collections at the British Library: the record of a life well read.

READING ROOM

READING ROOM

A Year of Literary Curiosities

SELECTED BY
IAN SANSOM

BRITISH LIBRARY

This edition published 2019 by
The British Library
96 Euston Road
London NW1 2DB

Selection and introduction © 2019 Ian Sansom

Ian Sansom has asserted his right to be identified
as author of the Work

Cataloguing in Publication Data
A catalogue record for this book is
available from the British Library

ISBN 978 0 7123 5254 3

Front cover image: Japanese leaf print from the
Olga Hirsch decorated papers collection © The British
Library Board
All images and illustrations in this book are sourced from
the British Library collection © The British Library Board

The monthly chapter openers feature designs and details
from the decorated papers collection held at the British
Library.

Every effort has been made to trace copyright holders and
to obtain their permission for the use of copyright material.
A list of acknowledgements may be found facing the last
page in this collection. The publisher apologises for any
errors or omissions and would be pleased to be notified
of any corrections to be incorporated in reprints or future
editions.

Cover design by Blok Graphic
Designed and typeset by Jonny Davidson

Printed and bound in Malta by Gutenberg Press

❧ CONTENTS

Introduction

I started keeping the notes in my teens. When I read a book I would jot down passages and ideas that caught my attention: George Eliot, Tintin, Malcolm X. It didn't matter what it was: Julie Burchill in the *NME*, Christopher Ricks in *The Listener*, my first attempts at reading Proust, Rimbaud and Baudelaire. It became a habit. Week after week, and then month after month, and then years, and eventually decades of scribbling, for no purpose but for my own simple pleasure, and a desire perhaps not to forget, and to leave a trace: if not a life well lived, then at least a life well read.

I have hundreds of notebooks now, stacked high on shelves and crammed into drawers and mouldy old box files, filled to the brim with whatever I have managed to glean from the books and the magazines and the newspapers: the high and the low, and everything in between.

Most of the books have been library books – out of choice, and necessity. The beauty of library books is that you don't own them: they, briefly, own you. In a library, you are free to roam among the dross, and the first editions, and the oddities and the esoterica. Without libraries, my reading would not only have been restricted, it would have been entirely tamed.

My earliest hunting ground was our local library, an old demountable in a car park in Essex. Then there were the libraries in Romford and in Harlow, the college library, the big municipal and city libraries, and eventually the British Library, the national library – the largest, the greatest – with its many reading rooms. Here I found myself completely at home among the cranks and the hacks and the 'poverty-stricken scholars' who in Louis MacNeice's poem are famously busy 'cherishing their hobby or their doom'.[1]

---

1. The British Museum Reading-Room', in MacNeice, *The Collected Poems*, ed. E. R. Dodds, published in 1966, X.909/8789.

My own hobby, for my entire life, for better and for worse, has been to read widely, if not wisely, like those working class women readers described by Virginia Woolf, with some distaste, who set about their books 'with the indiscriminate greed of a hungry appetite, that crams itself with toffee and beef and tarts and vinegar and champagne all in one gulp'.[2]

Looking back at the evidence of my own wild feasting, certain themes and patterns emerge. There are authors, for example, whose work seems to have appealed to my tastes much more than others, and to whom I seem to have returned, again and again, year after year: Freud and Emerson, perhaps predictably, but also Ronald Knox and Rebecca West, Katherine Mansfield, Wodehouse, the Opies, Hannah Arendt. To my surprise, I seem to have read just about everything by Helen Waddell, absolutely everything by Barbara Kingsolver, and almost as much Wittgenstein as Agatha Christie. Like the wayward boy in Saki's story 'The Lumber-Room',[3] in among the chaos of my notes I have also discovered many fine old twisted candlesticks and bibelots that I had long since forgotten and consigned to oblivion. So many old cookbooks! The books on boxing! The celebrity bios and memoirs!

Among the forgotten treasures and the obvious patterns, I recognise also the many gaps and limitations. My knowledge of literature in languages other than English is poor, and my tastes and inclinations are inevitably those of a man of my age and background. All I can say in my defence is that I am not a scholar, that I do not pretend to any great learning or expertise, and that this Library Book, 366 readings selected from the holdings at the British Library (reproduced along with their shelfmarks), amounts to nothing but the commonplace book of a commonplace man with a very special library ticket.

Ian Sansom
2019

---

2. 'Introductory Letter' to *Life as We Have Known It*, published in association with the Women's Co-operative Guild in 1931, 08416.aaa.40.
3. in *The Short Stories of Saki* (1930), W20/5895.

JANUARY

 1 January

Off!

We are off!

Herman Melville,
Mardi and a voyage thither, etc. (1849)

012201.b.1/11,12

 2 January

A Definite Act

Landfall and Departure mark the rhythmical swing of a seaman's life and of a ship's career. From land to land is the most concise definition of a ship's earthly fate.

A 'Departure' is not what a vain people of landsmen may think. The term 'Landfall' is more easily understood; you fall in with the land, and it is a matter of a quick eye and of a clear atmosphere. The Departure is not the ship's going away from her port any more than the Landfall can be looked upon as the synonym of arrival. But there is this difference in the Departure: that the term does not imply so much a sea event as a definite act entailing a process – the precise observation of certain landmarks by means of the compass card.

Joseph Conrad,
The Mirror of the Sea: Memories and Impressions (1906)

C.116.bb.20

❧ 3 January ❧

What Makes Me Sad

[...] a person who has lived all his life in a certain city, and is finally compelled to move elsewhere, is, of course, saddened by the prospect of being thrown into a new environment – what is it, however, that actually makes him sad? It is not the prospect of leaving the place which was his home for long years, but the much more subtle fear of losing his very attachment to this place. What makes me sad is the fact that I am aware that, sooner or later – sooner than I am ready to admit – I will integrate myself into a new community, forgetting the place which now means so much to me. In short, what makes me sad is the awareness that I will lose my desire for (what is now) my home.

Slavoj Žižek, *Did Somebody Say Totalitarianism?* (2014)

ELD.DS.307470

 4 January

To Mark Gertler

Garsington
31 May 1916

Dearest Mark,

Your letter came this morning & filled me
with the uttermost sorrow because I know how miserable
you have been. It makes such a big gap & makes me realize
how little you believe in me. Do you not see an island in
the middle of a big lake, many islands of adventures which
one must swim across to? But one will <u>always</u> return to
the mainland. You are that mainland to me. I will leave
you sometimes perhaps. But always I shall come back and
when the best state of our friendship is arrived at, you will
love my adventures as you do your own. Mental & physical
adventures perhaps. Perhaps none. This world is so big &
full of surprises, but the great thing is, a simple faith in you
& a greater love for you than mankind. Do you never feel
the excitement of this big world & ships & many people?

Dora Carrington, *Carrington's Letters*,
ed. Anne Chisholm (2017)

ELD.DS.227517

🍂 5 January 🍂

The Minds of Young People

The minds of young people are pliable and elastic, and easily accommodate themselves to any one they fall in with. They find grounds of attraction both where they agree with one another and where they differ; what is congenial to themselves creates sympathy; what is correlative, or supplemental, creates admiration and esteem. And what is thus begun is often continued in after-life by the force of habit and the claims of memory. Thus, in the choice of friends, chance often does for us as much as the most careful selection could have effected.

John Henry Newman,
Loss and Gain: The Story of a Convert (1853)

1607/4044

🍂 6 January 🍂

What is the Difference?

Leave one man, marry another.
What is the difference?

Ama Ata Aidoo, *Changes* (1991)

H.91/965

 7 January

Arbitrariness

When will we grant arbitrariness the place it deserves in the creation of works or ideas? The things that touch us are generally less willed than we would believe. A felicitous expression or sensational discovery is announced in miserable fashion. Almost nothing achieves its goal, unless exceptionally, something surpasses it. And the history of these groupings – psychological literature – is hardly instructive: despite its pretensions, no novel has ever proven anything. The most illustrious examples of the genre are not worth setting before our eyes; the most appropriate response we could give it is total indifference. Unable as we are to embrace at once the entirety of a painting, or a misfortune, where do we get the right to judge?

André Breton, 'For Dada' (1920), in
The Lost Steps, trans. Mark Polizzotti (1996)

YC.1998.a.2513

 8 January

The Non-Necessity of It

Well: what we gain by science is, after all, sadness, as the Preacher saith. The more we know of the laws & nature of the Universe the more ghastly a business we perceive it all to be – & the non-necessity of it.

Thomas Hardy, letter to Edward Clodd, 27 February 1902, in
The Collected Letters of Thomas Hardy, eds Richard Little Purdy
and Michael Millgate, vol.3 (1982)

82/22663

9 January

A Coincidence!

'A coincidence! Here is one of the three men wh
named as possible actors in this drama, and he
violent death during the very hours when we k
drama was being enacted. The odds are enormo
its being a coincidence. No figures could express
my dear Watson, the two events are connected. I
to find the connection.'

Arthur Conan Doyle, 'The Adventure of the Secon
in *The Complete Sherlock Holmes* (1930)

012613.g.10

 10 January

The Veritable Characteristics of Chance

The greatest bit of chance is the birth of a great man. It is only by chance that meeting of two germinal cells, of different sex, containing precisely, each on its side, the mysterious elements whose mutual reaction must produce the genius. One will agree that these elements must be rare and that their meeting is still more rare. How slight a thing it would have required to deflect from its route the carrying spermatozoon. It would have sufficed to deflect it a tenth of a millimeter and Napoleon would not have been born and the destinies of a continent would have been changed. No example can better make us understand the veritable characteristics of chance.

Henri Poincaré, *The Foundations of Science: Science and Hypothesis, The Value of Science, Science and Method*, trans. George Bruce Halsted (1913; 1929)

501*760*

 11 January

Chance, When Strictly Examined

It is universally allowed that nothing exists without a cause of its existence, and that chance, when strictly examined, is a mere negative word, and means not any real power, which has anywhere a being in nature.

David Hume, *An Enquiry Concerning Human Understanding* (1748), ed. L. A. Selby-Bigge (1894)

8462.h.1

 12 January

Things Like These

Life is a question of nerves, and fibres, and slowly built-up cells in which thought hides itself and passion has its dreams. You may fancy yourself safe and think yourself strong. But a chance tone of colour in a room or a morning sky, a particular perfume that you had once loved and that brings subtle memories with it, a line from a forgotten poem that you had come across again, a cadence from a piece of music that you had ceased to play [...] I tell you, that it is on things like these that our lives depend.

Oscar Wilde, *The Picture of Dorian Gray* (1890);
unauthorised ed. with a false imprint, probably published in
London or Birmingham *c*.1904, the text taken from *Lippincott's
Monthly Magazine* for July 1890 with English spelling
substituted for American

X900/986

 13 January

I Tremble For My Ignorance

Once upon a time I held these beliefs about divorce: that everyone who does it could have chosen not to do it. That it's a lazy way out of marital problems. That it selfishly puts personal happiness ahead of family integrity. Now I tremble for my ignorance. It's easy, in fortunate times, to forget about the ambush that could leave your head reeling: serious mental or physical illness, death in the family, abandonment, financial calamity, humiliation, violence, despair. Disassembling a marriage in these circumstances is as much fun as amputating your own gangrenous leg. You do it, if you can, to save a life – or two, or more.

Barbara Kingsolver,
High Tide In Tucson: Essays From Now or Never (1996)
ELD.DS.125420

 14 January

To Be True to Oneself

Campaigners against [marriage], from Shelley and the Mills on, have been remarkably crass in posing the simple dilemma, 'either you want to stay together or you don't – if you do, you need not promise; if you don't, you ought to part.' This ignores the chances of inner conflict, and the deep human need for a continuous central life that lasts through genuine, but passing, changes of mood. The need to be able to rely on other people is not some sort of shameful weakness; it is an aspect of the need to be true to oneself.

Mary Midgley,
Beast and Man: The Roots of Human Nature (1979)
79/9188

15 January

This is the Saddest Story

For, whatever may be said of the relation of the sexes, there is no man who loved a woman that does not desire to come to her for the renewal of his courage, for the cutting asunder of his difficulties. And that will be the mainspring of his desire for her. We are all so afraid, we are all so alone, we all so need from the outside the assurance of our own worthiness to exist.

So, for a time, if such passion come to fruition, the man will get what he wants. He will get the moral support, the encouragement, the relief from the sense of loneliness, the assurance of his own worth. But these things pass away; inevitably they pass away as the shadows pass across sundials. It is sad, but it is so. The pages of the book will become familiar; the beautiful corner of the road will have been turned too many times. Well, this is the saddest story.

Ford Madox Ford, *The Good Soldier: A Tale of Passion*
(1915; 1927 edition)
72/20666

16 January

Oh! Well!

The years that are gone seem like dreams – if one might go on sleeping and dreaming – but to wake up and find – oh! well! Perhaps it is better to wake up after all, even to suffer, rather than to remain a dupe to illusions all one's life.

Kate Chopin, *The Awakening* (1899)
MFR-3052 *765* reel C-22

17 January

Time to Say No

When people ask for time, it's always for time to say no.
Yes has one more letter in it, but it doesn't take half as long
to say.

Edith Wharton, *The Children* (1928)

12714.dd.7

18 January

The Woman Adventurer

The Woman Adventurer – I employ the term in its narrowest
interpretation – is, in this age of universal freedom for
woman, likely to become extinct. At first sight such a
statement may seem absurd, but a closer inspection of the
terms will prove its truth. The Woman Adventurer is not
a woman who has achieved some heroic deed (whether in
men's clothes or not), nor yet the woman who has yielded
to some single strange freak and left the beaten track for
a little time; far from this, she is the woman with one
inherent, dominating passion for adventure, for change,
for surprise; the woman who keenly loves to be overtaken
by unexpected situations; who dotes on predicaments, who
revels in mischance. When do we hear of such a woman
to-day? Never. [...] Search for her just now, fine female
blusterer that she is, through the length and breadth of
England, and I warrant she will not be found.

Ménie Muriel Dowie, ed., *Women Adventurers: The Lives of
Madame Velazquez, Hannah Snell, Maryanne Talbot and
Mrs Christian Davies* (1893)

012207.k.1/15

 19 January

Written with a Diamond

In her imprisonment at Woodstock, these verses she wrote with her diamond in a glass window:

> Much suspected by me,
> Nothing proved can be.
> *Quod* Elizabeth the prisoner

Queen Elizabeth I, *Elizabeth I: Collected Works*,
eds Leah S. Marcus, Janet Mueller, and Mary Beth Rose (2000)

moo/34364

 20 January

The Predicament She Had Sought

She turned this way and that in the predicament she had sought and from which she could neither retreat with grace nor emerge with credit; she draped herself in the tatters of her impudence, postured to her utmost before the last little triangle of cracked glass to which so many fractures had reduced the polished plate of filial superstition.

Henry James, *What Maisie Knew* (1897; 1898)

012706.m.58

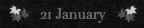 21 January

The Wrong Ditch

I returned from the City about three o'clock on that May afternoon pretty well disgusted with life. I had been three months in the Old Country, and was fed up with it. If anyone had told me a year ago that I would have been feeling like that I should have laughed at him; but there was the fact. The weather made me liverish, the talk of the ordinary Englishman made me sick, I couldn't get enough exercise, and the amusements of London seemed as flat as soda-water that has been standing in the sun. 'Richard Hannay,' I kept telling myself, 'you have got into the wrong ditch, my friend, and you had better climb out.'

John Buchan, *The Thirty-Nine Steps* (1915)

12601.ccc.25

 22 January

You're Only a Woman

17 April [1899] [Manchester]

I come back dead tired. As I sink into the armchair in
my little lodging the old maid lodging-house keeper says
exultantly: 'See, you are completely knocked up. You're
only a woman: in spite of your manly brain, you're just as
much of a woman as I am.' Poor genteel celibate! For days
back you have been envying me my energy, and peering
into Life and Labour on my table with my name standing
out as a contributor. Still more, you have been reading the
leaders in two London papers sent me by friends and you
have been hardly able to contain yourself with silent envy.
Now you have your revenge as I roll, tipsy with fatigue, up to
bed. 'You're only a woman after all,' I hear her mutterings
as she collars my bag to save my exertion, feeling herself
for once a superior. 'Poor weak woman with a man's brain,'
adds the old maid, trying to define the exact nature of her
distinguished lodger.

Beatrice Webb, *The Diary of Beatrice Webb*, vol.1,
Glitter Around: Darkness Within, 1873–1892,
eds Norman and Jeanne Mackenzie (1982)

82/29144

 23 January

As Profound as Hunger for Food

By the majority of 'nice' people woman is supposed to
have no spontaneous sex-impulses. By this I do not mean a
sentimental 'falling in love', but a physical, a physiological

state of stimulation which arises spontaneously and quite apart from any particular man. It is in truth the creative impulse, and is an expression of a high power of vitality. So widespread in our country is the view that it is only depraved women who have such feelings (especially before marriage) that most women would rather die than own that they do at times feel a physical yearning indescribable, but as profound as hunger for food. Yet many, many women have shown me the truth of their natures when I have simply and naturally assumed that of course they feel it – being normal women – and have asked them only: When? From their replies I have collected facts which are sufficient to overturn many ready-made theories about women.

Marie Stopes, *Married Love* (1919)

W22/5628

 24 January

The Natural Variations of Love

Now, having regard to the natural variations of love, I must suggest that the stigma must be removed from those who are not capable of lifelong fidelity. [...] One would imagine that the men who refuse to alter the divorce laws really do believe in the sacrament of the marriage ceremony, instead of in the sacrament of the true love, which abides when there is a real compatibility of temperament.

Florence Farr, *Modern Woman: Her Intentions* (1910)

08415.df.8

25 January

Merely Sensual Relations

Since we do not positively blame a man for remaining
celibate [...] it is difficult to show why we should condemn
– in its bearing on the individual's emotional perfection
solely – the imperfect development afforded by merely
sensual relations.

Henry Sidgwick, *The Methods of Ethics* (1874)
W14/4024

 26 January

A Gentil Cok

I have a gentil cok,
Crowyt me day;
He doth me rysyn erly,
My matyins for to say.

I have a gentil cok,
Comyn he is of gret;
His comb is of reed corel,
His tayil is of get.

I have a gentyl cok,
Comyn he is of kynde;
His comb is of red corel,
His tayl is of inde.

His legges ben of asor,
So gentil and so smale;
His spores arn of sylver qwyt,
Into the wortewale.

His eynyn arn of cristal,
Lokyn al in aumbry;
And every nyght he perchit hym
In myn ladyis chaumbyr.

British Library Sloane MS 2593, fol.10v; in *Secular Lyrics of the XIVth and XVth Centuries*, ed. Rossell Hope Robbins (1952)

11626.l.15

 27 January

Midling Pricks

Katy. Well, what say you to the midling Pricks?
Frank. They are from six to Nine Inches, they fit Women to a hair, and tickle them sweetly. As in Men so in Women too, there are great, small and midling Cunts, but when all is done be they little or great, there is nothing so precious as a friend's Prick that we love well, and though it be no longer then ones little finger, we find more satisfaction in it then in a longer of another mans. A well sized Prick must be reasonable big, but bigger at the Belly then at the Top, there is a sort of Prick I have not yet mentioned, called the Belly Prick, which is generally esteemed above the rest; It appears like a snail out of it's shell, and stands oftner than those large Tarses which are unweldy ladders, which take a great more time to Rear then little Ones.

Michel Millot and Jean L'Ange, *The School of Venus, Or The Ladies Delight, Reduced into Rules of Practice* (1680), trans. Donald Thomas (1972)

P.C.30.a.38

 28 January

The O'erpowering Sight

Now thou has seen my heart. Was it too near?
Didst thou recoil from the o'erpowering sight;
That vision of a scarred and seamed soul?
Ah! Yes: thy gentle eyes were filled with fear
When looks and thoughts broke out from my controul,
Bursting themselves a road with fiercest might –
Wide open secret cells of foulest sin,
And all that lurks in that dark place within!

Frederick William Faber, from 'The Confessional',
The Cherwell Water Lily: And Other Poems (1840)

993.d.14

🍁 29 January 🍁

To Limp

If mimetic rivalry plays an essential role in the Gospels, how does it happen, you may object, that Jesus does not put us on guard against it? Actually he does put us on guard, but we don't know it. When what he says contradicts our illusions, we ignore him.

The words that designate mimetic rivalry and its consequences are the noun *skandalon* and the verb *skandalizein*. Like the Hebrew word that it translates, 'scandal' means not one of those ordinary obstacles that we avoid easily after we run into it the first time, but a paradoxical obstacle that is almost impossible to avoid: the more this obstacle, or scandal, repels us, the more it attracts us. Those who are scandalized put all the more ardour in injuring themselves against it because they were injured there before.

The Greek word *skandalizein* comes from a verb that means 'to limp.' What does a lame person resemble? To someone following a person limping it appears that the person continually collides with his or her own shadow.

René Girard, *I See Satan Fall Like Lightning*,
trans. James G. Williams (2001)

YC.2001.a.9130

 30 January

I Learnt the Truth

I am a ridiculous person. Now they call me a madman. That would be a promotion if it were not that I remain as ridiculous in their eyes as before. But now I do not resent it, they are all dear to me now, even when they laugh at me – and indeed, it is just then that they are particularly dear to me. I could join in their laughter – not exactly at myself, but through affection for them, if I did not feel so sad as I look at them. Sad because they do not know the truth and I do know it. Oh, how hard it is to be the only one who knows the truth! But they won't understand that. No, they won't understand it. [...] I learnt the truth last November – on the third of November, to be precise – and I remember every instant since. It was a gloomy evening, one of the gloomiest possible evenings. I was going home at about eleven o'clock, and I remember that I thought that the evening could not be gloomier. Even physically. Rain had been falling all day, and it had been a cold, gloomy, almost menacing rain, with, I remember, an unmistakable spite against mankind. Suddenly between ten and eleven it had stopped, and was followed by a horrible dampness, colder and damper than the rain, and a sort of steam was rising from everything, from every stone in the street, and from every by-lane if one looked down it as far as one could. A thought suddenly occurred to me, that if all the street lamps had been put out it would have been less cheerless, that the gas made one's heart sadder because it lighted it all up.

 31 January

Knowledge, the Juggernaut

What a grown man worships is truth – knowledge – science – light – the rending of the veil and the pushing back of the shadow. Knowledge, the juggernaut! There is death in our own ritual. We must kill – dissect – destroy – and all for the sake of discovery – the worship of the ineffable light. The goddess Science demands it. We test a doubtful poison by killing. How else? No thought for self – just knowledge – the effect must be known.

H. P. Lovecraft and Adolphe de Castro, 'The Last Test',
in *Weird Tales*, November 1928

YC.2001.a.9130

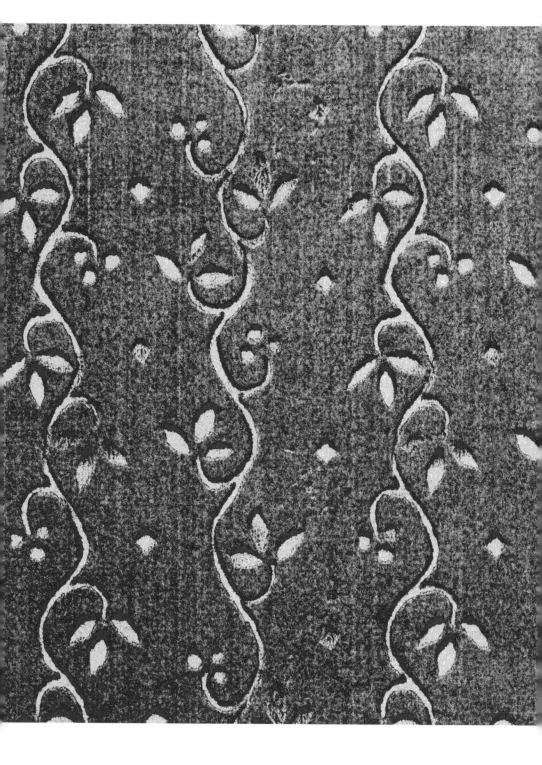

FEBRUARY

1 February

Marionette Players

And now, I said, let me show in a figure how far our nature is enlightened or unenlightened: Behold! Human beings living in an underground den, which has a mouth open towards the light and reaching all along the den; here they have been from their childhood, and have their legs and necks chained so that they cannot move, and can only see before them, being prevented by the chains from turning round their heads. Above and behind them a fire is blazing at a distance, and between the fire and the prisoners there is a raised way; and you will see, if you look, a low wall built along the way, like the screen which marionette players have in front of them, over which they show the puppets.

Plato, *The Republic*, c.380 BCE,
trans. Benjamin Jowett (1888)

2280.d.14

2 February

A Machine for the Making of Gods

Men do not sufficiently realize that their future is in their own hands. Theirs is the task of determining first of all whether they want to go on living or not. Theirs the responsibility, then, for deciding if they want merely to live, or intend to make just the extra effort required for fulfilling, even on their refractory planet, the essential function of the universe, which is a machine for the making of gods.

Henri Bergson, *The Two Sources of Morality and Religion* [1932],
trans. R. Ashley Audra and Cloudesley Brereton

170 *2157*

✣ 3 February ✣

Something Gorgeous About Him

If personality is an unbroken series of successful gestures, then there was something gorgeous about him, some heightened sensitivity to the promises of life, as if he were related to one of those intricate machines that register earthquakes ten thousand miles away.

F. Scott Fitzgerald, *The Great Gatsby* (1925)

Cup.406.i.13

✣ 4 February ✣

And Yet I Am

I am – yet what I am, none cares or knows;
    My friends forsake me like a memory lost: –
I am the self-consumer of my woes –
    They rise and vanish in oblivious host
Like shadows in love's frenzied stifled throes
And yet I am, and live – like vapours tossed

Into the nothingness of scorn and noise,
    Into the living sea of waking dreams,
Where there is neither sense of life or joys,
    But the vast shipwreck of my life's esteems;
Even the dearest, that I loved the best
Are strange – nay, rather, stranger than the rest.

I long for scenes where man hath never trod
    A place where woman never smiled or wept
There to abide with my Creator, God,
    And sleep as I in childhood sweetly slept,
Untroubling and untroubled where I lie
The grass below – above the vaulted sky.

John Clare, 'I Am!',
in *Poems by John Clare*, ed. Arthur Symons (1908)
Bloomfield 280

5 February

A Sense of Power

The afternoon slipped away almost without Joe's knowledge. He walked about here and there, gazing with curious eyes at the streets and warehouses and passing vehicles, and thinking what a lively place New York was, and how different life was in the metropolis from what it had been to him in the quiet country town which had hitherto been his home. Somehow it seemed to wake Joe up and excite his ambition, to give him a sense of power which he had never felt before.

Horatio Alger, *Joe's Luck* (1900)
X.998/881

6 February

The Veil of Color

The worlds within and without the Veil of Color are changing and changing rapidly, but not at the same rate, not in the same way; and this must produce a peculiar wrenching of the soul, a peculiar sense of doubt and bewilderment. Such a double life, with double thought, double duties and double social classes, must give rise to double words and double ideals, and temple the mind to pretence or to revolt, to hypocrisy or to radicalism.

W. E. B. Du Bois, *The Souls of Black Folk* (1903)

8157.df.9

The Filmiest of Screens

One conclusion was forced upon my mind at that time, and my impression of its truth has ever remained unshaken. It is that our normal waking consciousness, rational consciousness as we call it, is but one special type of consciousness, whilst all about it, parted from it by the filmiest of screens, there lie potential forms of consciousness entirely different. We may go through life without suspecting their existence; but apply the requisite stimulus, and at a touch they are all there in all their completeness [...] Looking back on my own experiences, they all converge towards a kind of insight to which I cannot help ascribing some metaphysical significance. The keynote of it is invariably a reconciliation. It is as if the opposites of the world, who contradictoriness and conflict make all our difficulties and troubles, were melted into unity.

William James, *The Varieties of Religious Experience: A Study in Human Nature* (1902)

415.260000 1901–1902

❦ 8 February ❧

The Noise of the Gramophone Within

Eternity is with us, inviting our contemplation perpetually, but we are too frightened, lazy, and suspicious to respond; too arrogant to still our thought, and let divine sensation have its way. It needs industry and goodwill if we would make that transition; for the process involves a veritable spring-cleaning of the soul, a turning-out and rearrangement of our mental furniture, a wide opening of closed windows, that the notes of the wild birds beyond our garden may come to us fully charged with wonder and freshness, and drown with their music the noise of the gramaphone within. Those who do this, discover that they have lived in a stuffy world, whilst their inheritance was a world of morning-glory; where every tit-mouse is a celestial messenger, and every thrusting bud is charged with the full significance of life.

Evelyn Underhill, *Practical Mysticism:*
A Little Book for Normal People (1914)

08462.e.18

❦ 9 February ❧

Fairy-Tale Time

We are travelling to the Paris Exhibition.

Now we are there! it was a flight, a rush, but quite without witchcraft; we came by steam, in a ship and on a high road.

Our time is the fairy-tale time.

We are in the midst of Paris, in a great hotel, all the staircase is decorated with flowers, and soft carpets cover the steps.

Hans Christian Andersen, 'The Dryad' (1868),
in *Fairy Tales and Other Stories by Hans Christian Andersen*,
eds William Alexander Craigie and
Jessie Kinmond Craigie (1914)

12410.df.21

❧ 10 February ☙

Second Hand Delights

To ALL THOSE WHO LEAD MONOTONOUS LIVES
in the hope that they may experience at second hand the
delights and dangers of adventure.

Agatha Christie, dedication to *The Secret Adversary* (1922)

H.95/3451

❧ 11 February ☙

The Helping Hands

No radiant angel came across the gloom with a clear message
for her. In those times, as now, there were human beings
who never saw angels or heard perfectly clear messages.
Such truth as came to them was brought confusedly in
the voices and deeds of men not at all like the seraphs of
unfailing wing and piercing vision [...] The helping hands
stretched out to them were the hands of men who stumbled
and often saw dimly, so that these beings unvisited by
angels had no other choice than to grasp the stumbling
guidance along the path of reliance and action which is
the path of life, or else to pause in loneliness and disbelief,
which is no path, but the arrest of inaction and death.

George Eliot, *Romola* (1863)

12654.b.15

 12 February

Midnight is Nigh

The Moon and Pleiades have set,
Midnight is nigh,
The time is passing, passing, yet
Alone I lie.

Sappho, in
Sappho: The Poems and Fragments,
ed. C. R. Haines (1926)

L.R.34.a.1/41

❦ 13 February ❧

The Silent Hour of Night

I love the silent hour of night,
For blissful dreams may then arise,
Revealing to my charmed sight
What may not bless my waking eyes!

And then a voice may meet my ear
That death has silenced long ago;
And hope and rapture may appear
Instead of solitude and woe.

Cold in the grave for years has lain
The form it was my bliss to see,
And only dreams can bring again
The darling of my heart to me.

Anne Brontë, 'The Silent Hour of Night',
in *Brontë Poems*, ed. A. C. Benson (1915)

11641.aa.61

14 February

The Stored-Up Love

Love is a joint experience between two persons – but the fact that it is a joint experience does not mean that it is a similar experience to the two people involved. There are the lover and the beloved, but these two come from different countries. Often the beloved is only a stimulus for all the stored-up love which has lain quiet within the lover for a long time hitherto.

Carson McCullers,
The Ballad of the Sad Café (1951; 1963 edn)
H.2000/1349

15 February

Take Two Large and Tender Hearts

How to Make an Ordinary Love Poem: Take two large and tender human hearts, which match one another perfectly. Arrange these close together, but preserve them from actual contact by placing between them some cruel barrier. Wound them both in several places, and insert through the openings thus made a fine stuffing of wild yearnings, hopeless tenderness, and a general admiration for stars. Then completely cover up one heart with a sufficient quantity of chill church-yard mould, which may be garnished according to taste with dank waving weeds or tender violets: and promptly break it over the other heart.

W. H. Mallock, 'A Newdigate Prizeman',
*Every Man His Own Poet: or,
The Inspired Singer's Recipe Book* (1872)
11825.bbb.7

❦ 16 February ❧

Ah My Dear

Last night, there was a moment before you got into bed. You stood, quite naked, bending forward a little – talking. It was only for an instant. I saw you – I loved you so – loved your body with such tenderness – Ah my dear – And I am not thinking now of 'passion'. No, of that other thing that makes me feel that every inch of you is so precious to me. Your soft shoulders – your creamy warm skin, your ears, cold like shells are cold – your long legs & your feet that I love to clasp with my feet – the feeling of your belly – & your think young back – Just below that bone that sticks out at the back of your neck you have a little mole. It is partly because we are young that I feel this tenderness – I love your youth – I could not bear that it should be touched even by a cold wind if I were the Lord.

We two, you know have everything before us, and we shall do very great things – I have perfect faith in us – and so perfect is my love for you that I am, as it were, still, silent to my very soul. I want nobody but you for my lover and my friend and to nobody but you shall I be *faithful*.

I am yours for ever

Tig.

Katherine Mansfield, letter to John Middleton Murray, 18 May 1917, in *The Collected Letters of Katherine Mansfield*, eds Vincent O'Sullivan and Margaret Scott (1984)

YC.2008.a.10924 vol. 5

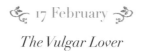

The Vulgar Lover

Evil is the vulgar lover who loves the body rather than the soul, inasmuch as he is not even stable, because he loves a thing which is in itself unstable, and therefore when the bloom of youth which he was desiring is over, he takes wing and flies away, in spite of all his words and promises; whereas the love of the noble disposition is life-long, for it becomes one with the everlasting.

Plato, 'Symposium', *c.*385–370 BCE, in *The Dialogues of Plato,*
vol.I, trans. Benjamin Jowett (1868)
C.194.b.61

18 February

The Poor Scanty Pittance of It

I would rather be a man of disinterested taste and liberal feeling, to see and acknowledge truth and beauty wherever I found it, than a man of greater and more original genius, to hate, envy and deny all excellence but my own – but that poor scanty pittance of it (compared with the whole) which I had myself produced!

William Hazlitt, 'On Criticism',
in *Table Talk: Or, Original Essays* (1821)
629.e.20

❧ 19 February ☙

He Notes with a Smile

The work of a publisher's reader cultivates his sense of irony.
He sees so many writers start, so many men of promise never
arrive, perhaps for lack of encouragement. He witnesses
the daily triumph of the mediocrities, hailed everywhere
by the mediocre, the success of the adroit shallow talents
quickly staled by the years. He watches the literary cliques
at work, each loyally championing its members. He notes
with a smile the pressmen rushing to acclaim the work of
a writer suddenly grown popular, whose finest effort, ten
years back, was greeted with chilling or patronising nods.
He sees also the force or fire of the finest craftsmen finally
prevail, and the day of other fine talents dawning. The
publisher's reader knows what literary success signifies: he
has no need to cultivate his sense of irony.

Edward Garnett, preface to
Friday Nights: Literary Criticisms and Appreciations (1929)
W 8/849

20 February

Here is Truth

Fate must have her joke sometimes, as well as the least of us, and she suffers cheap energy to fill the newspapers for a lustrum, and genius to await identification at the morgue. These are truisms, but here is truth: in nine hundred and ninety-nine instances out of a thousand, it is folly to name any success or failure as such; for either is a mystery, and the fairest evidences by which we can form an opinion of it are altogether and irremediably fallacious.

Louise Imogen Guiney, 'The Underdog' (1893), in
Patrins (1895)

012356.ee.44

21 February

Moral Flabbiness

[...] the moral flabbiness born of the exclusive worship of the bitch-goddess SUCCESS. That – with the squalid cash interpretation put on the word 'success' – is our national disease.

William James, letter to H. G. Wells, 11 September 1906,
in *The Letters of William James*,
ed. Henry James, vol.2 (1920)

W46/9667

22 February

Opulence in Evidence

Conspicuous consumption of valuable goods is a means of reputability to the gentleman of leisure. As wealth accumulates on his hands, his own unaided effort will not avail to sufficiently put his opulence in evidence by this method. The aid of friends and competitors is therefore brought in by resorting to the giving of valuable presents and expensive feasts and entertainments.

Thorstein Veblen,
The Theory of the Leisure Class (1899; 2nd edn 1912)
339 *4825*

23 February

Money is the Instrument

The Thermometer is the instrument for measuring the heat of the weather: the Barometer the instrument for measuring the pressure of the Air. Those who are not satisfied with the accuracy of those instruments must find out others that shall be more accurate, or bid adieu to Natural Philosophy. Money is the instrument of measuring the quantity of pain or pleasure. Those who are not satisfied with the accuracy of this instrument must find out some other that shall be more accurate, or bid adieu to politics and morals.

Jeremy Bentham, 'The Philosophy of Economic Science' (1793),
in *Jeremy Bentham's Economic Writings*,
ed. Werner Stark, vol.1 (1952)
08207.11.32

24 February

A Sound Banker

A 'sound' banker, alas! is not one who foresees danger and avoids it, but one who, when he is ruined, is ruined in a conventional and orthodox way along with his fellows, so that no one can really blame him.

John Maynard Keynes, 'The Consequences to the Banks of the Collapse of Money Values', in *Essays in Persuasion* (1933)

8224.pp.1

25 February

The Meaning of the Word 'Rich'

Primarily, which is very notable and curious, I observe that men of business rarely know the meaning of the word 'rich.' At least if they know, they do not in their reasonings allow for the fact, that it is a relative word, implying its opposite 'poor' as positively as the word 'north' implies its opposite 'south.' Men nearly always speak and write as if riches were absolute, and it were possible, by following certain scientific precepts, for everybody to be rich. Whereas riches are a power like that of electricity, acting only through inequalities or negations of itself. The force of the guinea you have in your pocket depends wholly on the default of a guinea in your neighbour's pocket. If he did not want it, it would be of no use to you; the degree of power it possesses depends accurately upon the need or desire he has for it,—and the art of making yourself rich, in the ordinary mercantile economist's sense, is therefore equally and necessarily the art of keeping your neighbour poor.

John Ruskin, 'The Veins of Wealth', in *Unto This Last* (1862)

8206.a.37

26 February

The Way to Bet

The race is not always to the swift nor the battle to the strong – but that's the way to bet.

Damon Runyon, *More Than Somewhat* (1937)

A.N.3685

27 February

The Folded Lie

All I have is a voice
To undo the folded lie,
The romantic lie in the brain
Of the sensual man-in-the-street
And the lie of Authority
Whose buildings grope the sky:
There is not such thing as the State
And no one exists alone;
Hunger allows no choice
To the citizen or the police;
We must love one another or die.

W. H. Auden, from 'September 1, 1939',
in *Another Time* (1940)

11656.e.24

❧ 28 February ❧

Hope of Rest, Hope of Product, Hope of Pleasure

Here, you see, are two kinds of work – one good, the other bad; one not far removed from a blessing, a lightening of life; the other a mere curse, a burden to life.

What is the difference between them, then? This: one has hope in it, the other has not. It is manly to do the one kind of work, and manly also to refuse to do the other.

What is the nature of the hope which, when it is present in work, makes it worth doing?

It is threefold, I think – hope of rest, hope of product, hope of pleasure in the work itself; and hope of these also in some abundance and of good quality; rest enough and good enough to be worth having; product worth having by one who is neither a fool nor an ascetic; pleasure enough for all of us to be conscious of it while we are at work; not a mere habit, the loss of which we shall feel as a fidgety man feels the loss of the bit of string he fidgets with.

William Morris, *Useful Work Versus Useless Toil* (1885)

Cup.502.f.11.(25.)

❧ 29 February ❧

An Artist of True Feeling

Art is nothing but a natural result of man's organization, which is of such a nature that he derives particular pleasure from certain combinations of forms, lines, colours, movements, sounds, rhythms and images. But these combinations only give him pleasure when they express the sentiments and emotions of the human soul struggling with the accidents of life, or in presence of scenes of nature.

[...] An artist of true feeling has but to abandon himself to his emotion and it will become contagious, and the praise that he deserves will be awarded to him. So long as he shall observe the positive rules that spring from the physiological necessities of our organs, and which alone are certain and definitive, he need never trouble himself about academic traditions and receipts. He is free, absolutely free in his own province, on the one condition of absolute sincerity. He must seek only to express the ideas, sentiments and emotions proper to himself, and must copy no one.

Eugène Véron, *Aesthetics*, trans. W. H. Armstrong (1879)

2244.d.12

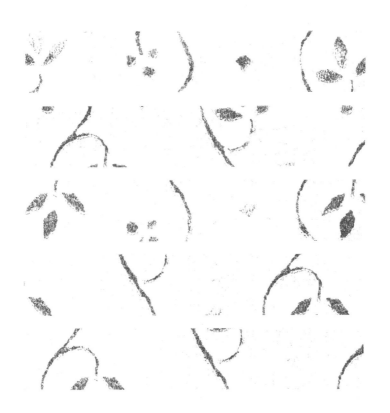

MARCH

MOLOSSO

 1 March

Annihilating Time

Imagination is no more than the making of graven images, whether of things on the earth or in the mind. To make them, clear concentrated sight and patient mind are the most necessary things after love; and those two are the children of love. With the majority, love, accompanying and giving birth to imagination, reaches its intensity only once, and that briefly in a lifetime; and if they are ever again to know imagination, it is through fear, as when a tall flame shoots up before the eyes, or through sudden pain or anger giving their faces an honest energy of expression, and their lips, perhaps, a power of telling speech. Yet more rare is the power of repeating those images by music or language or carved stone. It is those who can do so who alone are, as a rule, aware that human life, nature, and art are every moment continuing and augmenting the Creation – making to-day the first day, and this field Eden, annihilating time – so that each moment all things are fresh and the sun has not drunken the blessed dew from off their bloom. The seeing eye of child or lover, the poet's verse, the musician's melody, add thus continually to the richness of the universe. Jefferies early possessed such an eye, such an imagination, though not for many years could he reveal some of its images by means of words. In fact, he was very soon to bear witness to the pitiful truth that the imagination does not supply the words that shall be its expression; he was to fill much paper with words that revealed almost nothing of his inner and little more of his outer life.

Edward Thomas,
Richard Jefferies: His Life and Work (1909)

010827.g.30

 2 March

A Little Book in Such a Mode

When at the first I took my Pen in hand
Thus for to write, I did not understand
That I at all should make a little Book
In such a mode; Nay, I had undertook
To make another, which when almost done,
Before I was aware I this begun.

John Bunyan, from 'The Author's Apology for his Book', in
The Pilgrim's Progress (1678; photographic reproduction of
first edn, 1931)
L.R.263.a.1

 3 March

What are Master-pieces?

What are master-pieces and why after all are there so few of
them. You may say after all there are a good many of them
but in any kind of proportion with everything that anybody
who does anything is doing there are really very few of
them. All this summer I meditated and wrote about this
subject and it finally came to be a discussion of the relation
of human nature and the human mind and identity. The
thing one gradually comes to find out is that one has no
identity that is when one is in the act of doing anything.
Identity is recognition, you know who you are because
you and others remember anything about yourself but
essentially you are not that when you are doing anything.
I am I because my little dog knows me but, creatively

speaking the little dog knowing that you are you and your recognizing that he knows, that is what destroys creation. This is what makes school. Picasso once remarked I do not care who it is that has or does influence me as long as it is not myself. [...] Therefore a master-piece has essentially not to be necessary, it has to be that is it has to exist but it does not have to be necessary it is not in response to necessity as action is because the minute it is necessary it has in it no possibility of going on.

Gertrude Stein, from 'What Are Master-pieces and Why Are There So Few of Them', in *What are Master-pieces?* (1940)

11863.d.12

4 March

It is Clear

Es ist klar, dass sich die Ethik nicht aussprechen laesst.
Die Ethik ist transzendental.
(Ethik und Aesthetik sind eins.)

It is clear that ethics cannot be expressed.
Ethics is transcendental.
(Ethics and aesthetics are one.)

Ludwig Wittgenstein,
Tractatus Logico-Philosophicus [1921], trans. C. K. Ogden (1922)

8458.s.1/4

5 March

When We Have Crossed the Threshold

A stained glass window is itself the best possible illustration of the difference it makes whether we look at a thing from this side or that. Goethe used this particular image in one his little parables, comparing poems to painted windows, dark and dull from the market-place, bright with colour and alive with meaning only when we have crossed the threshold of the church.

Lewis F. Day,
Windows: A Book About Stained and Painted Glass (1897)
W23/7780

6 March

The Color Sense

Ruskin was right when he said that anyone could learn to draw – he was himself an admirable draughtsman – but only those who were to the manner born could become colorists. For the color sense, like the musical sense, appears to be a gift, and though amenable to training and development in everyone, it is so only within limits which the born colorist – like the born composer in the field of music – will easily overpass.

Claude Bragdon, *The Frozen Fountain:*
Being Essays on Architecture and the Art of Design in Space
(1924; 1932 edn)
7822.b.43

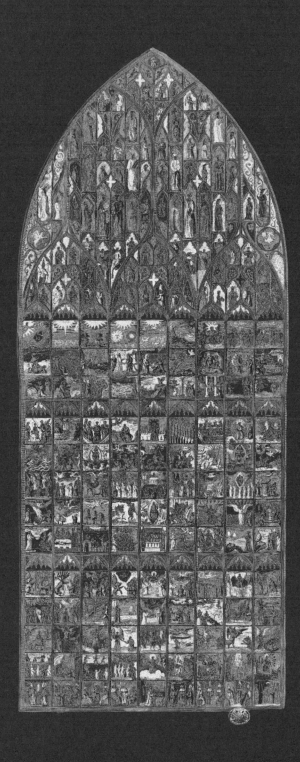

❧ 7 March ☙

A Compromise – Pshaw

'You ask me how much the public should be considered, and I say, not at all.'

My eyebrows must have gone up, for Mr. Moore added, 'You disagree?'

'In part,' I replied, 'for I have always imagined some kind of a compromise between earth and heaven.'

'A compromise – pshaw – Why a compromise? [...] a writer must set out to please the public? And if he please them to be sure the public will applaud, and if he please them more, and he will certainly try, the public will applaud more. And when when the public is tired, the public kicks him out, that is all.' [...]

'And so your advice ...', I said.

'My advice, no, no, no.'

'Your counsel?'

'No, neither advice, nor counsel, nor precept would I give. This is the greatest fallacy of all. One simply cannot advise anyone. They will do good work or they will do bad work. They may go with the stream or they may go against it. But neither do they do on advice nor counsel. Everyone does what he can. That is almost the only thing on which we can be anything like definite. It is a mistake to imagine people write badly to get the public; it is a mistake to imagine a man writes over the public because he thinks this is as it should be. The man who writes for the public, and the man who turns his back on the public, are doing what they were meant to do. There is no more that can be said.'

'And the man who turns his back on the public, should not be commended for his courage?' I replied.

'No, why should he? He is merely being himself as each one of the other ninety-nine might also say.'

Geraint Goodwin, *Conversations with George Moore* (1929)

010855.ee.38

🌸 8 March 🌸

That Monotonous Brag

Ornament has primarily nothing to do with story, poetry, or other purpose than that which it sets itself – the purpose, that is to say, of ornamenting some given space or thing.

It may be quite true that ornament which does no more than this deserves no very high place in our esteem. The artist very naturally magnifies art; and to the craftsman craftsmanship is of the first importance; but to him only. To mankind in general it is the man behind the art that interests them; and the Philistine is not such a fool, after all, in asking of the artist who claims his attention that he shall have something to say for himself. When the everlasting burden of his song is only, 'See what an artist I am!' we soon weary of that monotonous brag, even though it be warranted by some degree of achievement.

Lewis F. Day, *Nature in Ornament* (1892)

W79/6488

9 March

Their So Inept Performances

But when great and ingenious artists behold their so inept performances, not undeservedly do they ridicule the blindness of such men; since sane judgment abhors nothing so much as a picture perpetrated with no technical knowledge, although with plenty of care and diligence. Now the sole reason why painters of this sort are not aware of their own error is that they have not learnt Geometry, without which no one can either be or become an absolute artist; but the blame for this should be laid upon their masters, who are themselves ignorant of this art.

Albrecht Dürer, 'The Art of Measurement' (1525), in *Of the just shaping of letters. From the Applied geometry of Albrecht Dürer, book III.*, trans. R. T. Nichol (1917)

C.98.gg.11

 10 March

The Surface of Things

Our language is replete with the buried metaphors of such words as 'depth', and 'profundity' and 'weight', as terms of praise; and 'superficiality', 'lightness', etc., as terms of disparagement. They do not correspond to fact. The surface is the best thing to see. A lark sees more of the surface of the earth than the earthworm. For a broad view of anything we ought to need a 'superficial' man. In this way we talk of a 'weighty argument', as if argument should be as heavy as a bag of cement, whereas in reality good argument should be as light as a high explosive.

Stephen Leacock, *Humour and Humanity* (1917)

12199.p.1/210

⁂ 11 March ⁂

A Mere Figure of Speech

A part of the bourgeoisie is desirous of redressing social grievances in order to secure the continued existence of bourgeois society.

To this section belong economists, philanthropists, humanitarians, improvers of the condition of the working class, organisers of charity, members of societies for the prevention of cruelty to animals, temperance fanatics, hole-and-corner reformers of every imaginable kind. This form of socialism has, moreover, been worked out into complete systems...

The socialistic bourgeois want all the advantages of modern social conditions without the struggles and dangers necessarily resulting therefrom. They desire the existing state of society minus its revolutionary and disintegrating elements. They wish for a bourgeoisie without a proletariat. The bourgeoisie naturally conceives the world in which it is supreme to be the best; and bourgeois socialism develops this comfortable conception into various more or less complete systems. In requiring the proletariat to carry out such a system, and thereby to march straightway into the social New Jerusalem, it but requires in reality that the proletariat should remain within the bounds of existing society, but should cast away all its hateful ideas concerning the bourgeoisie...

Bourgeois socialism attains adequate expression when, and only when, it becomes a mere figure of speech.

Karl Marx and Friedrich Engels,
Manifesto of the Communist Party [1848],
trans. Samuel Moore (1888)

W3/3824-3839

 12 March

A Wide Fellow Feeling

All people of broad, strong sense have an instinctive repugnance to the men of maxims; because such people early discern that the mysterious complexity of our life is not to be embraced by maxims and that to lace ourselves up in formulas of that sort is to repress all the divine promptings and inspirations that spring from growing insight and sympathy. And the man of maxims is the popular representative of the minds that are guided in their moral judgment solely by general rules, thinking that these will lead them to justice by ready-made patent method, without the trouble of exerting patience, discrimination, impartiality, without any care to assure themselves whether they have the insight that comes from a hardly earned estimate of temptation or from a life vivid and intense enough to have created a wide fellow feeling with all that is human.

George Eliot, *The Mill on the Floss* (1860)

12633.f.12

 13 March

One Set of Catchwords

Man is a creature who lives not upon bread alone, but principally by catchwords; and the little rift between the sexes is astonishingly widened by simply teaching one set of catchwords to the girls and another to the boys.

Robert Louis Stevenson,
Virginibus Puerisque and Other Papers (1881)

W28/4054

14 March

Remarks

Remarks are not literature.

Gertrude Stein,
The Autobiography of Alice B. Toklas (1933)

20017.f.4

15 March

Like a Porcupine

A fragment, like a miniature work of art, has to be entirely isolated from the surrounding world and be complete in itself like a porcupine.

Friedrich Schleiermacher, *Schleiermacher's Soliloquies*,
trans. Horace Leland Friess (1926)

08466.de.42

✤ 16 March ✤

To Grow Weary of Preparation

I love anecdotes. I fancy mankind may come, in time, to write all aphoristically, except in narrative; grow weary of preparation, and connection, and illustration, and all those arts by which a big book is made.

James Boswell, *The Journal of a Tour to the Hebrides with Samuel Johnson* (1785)

567.c.16

✤ 17 March ✤

London Coffee-House Echo

It is folly to mistake the echo of a London coffee-house for the voice of the kingdom.

Jonathan Swift, *The Conduct of the Allies* (1763)

1485.l.1

18 March

elus(ive)(ory), illus(ive)(ory)

That is elusive which we fail, in spite of efforts, to grasp physically or mentally; the elusive ball, half-back, submarine; elusive rhythm, perfume, fame; an elusive image, echo, pleasure. That is illusory which turns out when attained to be unsatisfying, or which appears to be of more solid or permanent value than it really is; illusory fulfilment, success, victory, possession, promises.

The elusive mocks its pursuer, the illusory its possessor.

H. W. Fowler, *A Dictionary of Modern English Usage*,
2nd edition rev. Sir Ernest Gowers (1965)
T 20858

19 March

To Ridicule the Traveller

It is customary to ridicule the traveller who passes rapidly through a country, and then writes his impression of it. The truth is he sees much that is hidden for ever from the eyes of the inhabitants. Habit and custom have blinded them.

Olive Schreiner, *Thoughts on Africa* (1923)
X22/7600

 20 March

Where the Pickings Are

Adventurers, though, must take things as they find them,
  And look for pickings where the pickings are.

The drives of love and hunger are behind them,
  They can't afford to be particular:
And those who like good cooking and a car,

A certain kind of costume or of face,

Must seek them in a certain place.

W. H. Auden and Louis MacNeice, *Letters from Iceland* (1937)
010281.f.51

 21 March

Shifts and Contrivances Available in Wild Countries

The idea of the work occurred to me when exploring South-
western Africa in 1850–51. [...] Then remembering how
the traditional maxims and methods of travelling in each
country differ from those of others, and how every traveller
discovers some useful contrivances for himself, it appeared
to me, that I should do welcome service to all who have to
rough it, – whether explorers, emigrants, missionaries or
soldiers, – by collecting the scattered experiences of many
such persons in various circumstances, collating them,
examining into their principles, and deducing from them
what might fairly be called an 'Art of Travel.'

Blistered feet
To prevent the feet from blistering, it is a good plan to soap the inside of the stocking before setting out, making a thick lather all over it. A raw egg broken into a boot, before putting it on, greatly softens the leather.

[...]

Swimming with a horse
Lead him along a steep bank, and push him sideways, suddenly into the water: having fairly started him, jump in yourself, seize his tail, and let him tow you across. If he turns his head with the intention of changing his course, splash water in his face with your right or left hand, as the case may be, holding the tail with one hand and splashing with the other; and you will, in this way, direct him just as you like.

Keeping dogs at bay
A watching dog usually desists from flying at a stranger when he seats himself quietly on the ground, like Ulysses.

Francis Galton, *The Art of Travel: Or, Shifts and Contrivances Available in Wild Countries*, etc. (1855; fourth edn 1872)

10003.b.16

 22 March

All Truth is Practical

No truth is a saving truth – yes, no truth is a truth at all unless it guides and directs life. [...] There is no such thing as a purely intellectual form of assertion which has no element of action about it. An opinion is a deed. It is a deed intended to guide other deeds. It proposes to have what the pragmatists call 'workings.' That is, it undertakes to guide the life of the one who asserts the opinion. In that sense, all truth is practical.

Josiah Royce, *The Sources of Religious Insight. Lectures delivered before Lake Forest College on the foundation of the late William Bross (The Bross Lectures 1911)* (1912)

4374.b.37

 23 March

The Horizon of its Own Truths

We often think that the further an argument is developed (the more strongly elaborated and the more thoroughly exemplified) the more compelling it becomes. And while this result no doubt follows in one perspective, in another it does not follow at all. For when an argument seeks full self-development it begins to approach the horizon of its own truths, and hence begins to expose itself to disconfirmation and critique.

Jerome McGann, *Black Riders: The Visible Language of Modernism* (1993)

93/15827

 24 March

More Comprehensive Views

It is difficult to understand why statisticians commonly limit their equities to Averages, and do not revel in more comprehensive views. Their souls seem as dull to the charm of variety as that of the native of one of our flat English counties, whose retrospect of Switzerland was that, if its mountains could be thrown into its lakes, two nuisances would be got rid of at once. An average is but a solitary fact, whereas if a single other fact be added to it, an entire Normal Scheme, which nearly corresponds to the observed one, starts potentially into existence.

Francis Galton, *Natural Inheritance* (1889)

2255.f.17

❦ 25 March ❦

The Roar of a Ruthless Multitude

While you are young you will be oppressed, and angry, and increasingly disagreeable. When you reach middle age, at five-and-thirty, you will become complacent and, in your turn, an oppressor; those whom you oppress will find you still disagreeable; and so will all the people whose toes you trod upon in youth. It will seem to you then that you grow wiser every day, as you learn more and more of the reasons why things should not be done, and understand more fully the peculiarities of powerful persons, which make it quixotic even to attempt them without first going through an amount of squaring and lobbying sufficient to sicken any but the most hardened soul. If you persist to the threshold of old age – your fiftieth year, let us say – you will be a powerful person yourself, with an accretion of peculiarities which other people will have to study in order to square you. The toes you will have trodden on by this time will be as the sands on the sea-shore; and from far below you will mount the roar of a ruthless multitude of young men in a hurry. You may perhaps grow to be aware what they are in a hurry to do. They are in a hurry to get you out of the way.

F. M. Cornford, *Microcosmographia Academia:*
Being a Guide for the Young Academic Politician (1908)

X.809/4912.(1)

The Democracy of the Dead

Tradition means giving votes to the most obscure of all classes, our ancestors. It is the democracy of the dead. Tradition refuses to submit to the small and arrogant oligarchy of those who merely happen to be walking about. All democrats object to men being disqualified by the accident of birth; tradition objects to their being disqualified by the accident of death.

G. K. Chesterton, *Orthodoxy* (1908)

W 24/9200

27 March

The Denial of Life and Joy

I did not believe that a Cause which stood for a beautiful ideal, for anarchism, for release and freedom from conventions and prejudice, should demand the denial of life and joy. I insisted that our Cause could not expect me to become a nun and that the movement should not be turned into a cloister. If it meant that, I did not want it.

Emma Goldman, *Living My Life* (1931)

10885.bbb.15

28 March

One Element Which Makes the Crank

Cranks live by theory, not by pure desire. They want votes, peace, nuts, liberty, and spinning-looms not because they love these things, as a child loves jam, but because they think they ought to have them. That is one element which makes the crank.

Rose Macaulay, 'Cranks', in *A Casual Commentary* (1925)

X17/8567

🍂 29 March 🍂

The Thick and the Thin

Among the philosophic cranks of my acquaintance in the past was a lady all the tenets of whose system I have forgotten except one. Had she been born in the Ionian Archipelago some three thousand years ago, that one doctrine would probably have made her name sure of a place in every university curriculum and examination paper. The world, she said, is composed of only two elements, The Thick, namely, and The Thin. No one can deny the truth of this analysis, as far as it goes [...] and it is nowhere truer than in that part of the world called philosophy.

William James, *A Pluralistic Universe* (1909)
4303.550000 1909

✤ 3o March ✤

These Apertures, of Dissimilar Shape and Size

The house of fiction has in short not one window, but a million – a number of possible windows not to be reckoned, rather; every one of which has been pierced, or is still pierceable, in its vast front, by the need of the individual vision and by the pressure of the individual will. These apertures, of dissimilar shape and size, hang so, all together, over the human scene that we might have expected of them a greater sameness of report than we find. They are but windows at best, mere holes in a dead wall, disconnected, perched aloft; they are not hinged doors opening straight upon life. But they have this mark of their own that at each of them stands a figure with a pair of eyes, or at least with a field-glass, which forms, again and again, for observation, a unique instrument, insuring to the person making use of it an impression distinct from every other. He and his neighbors are watching the same show, but one seeing more where the other sees less, one seeing black where the other sees white, one seeing big where the other sees small, one seeing coarse where the other sees fine. And so on, and so on; there is fortunately no saying on what, for the particular pair of eyes, the window may not open; 'fortunately' by reason, precisely, of this incalculability of range. The spreading field, the human scene, is the 'choice of subject'; the pierced aperture, either broad or balconied or slit-like and low-browed, is the 'literary form'; but they are, singly or together, as nothing without the posted presence of the watcher – without, in other words, the consciousness of the artist. Tell me what the artist is, and I will tell you of what he has been conscious. Thereby I shall express to you at once his boundless freedom and his 'moral' reference.

Henry James, Preface to *The Portrait of a Lady* (1881), in *Novels and Stories*, vol.VI (1921)

12295.aaa

31 March

My Own Idea About Art

I have my own idea about art, and it is this: What most people regard as fantastic and lacking in universality, I hold to be the inmost essence of truth. Arid observation of everyday trivialities I have long since ceased to regard as realism – it is quite the reverse. In any newspaper one takes up, one comes across reports of wholly authentic facts, which nevertheless strike one as extraordinary. Our writers regard them as fantastic, and take no account of them; and yet they are the truth, for they are facts. But who troubles to observe, record, describe them? They happen every day and every moment, therefore they are not 'exceptional.'

Fyodor Dostoevsky, letter to Nikolay Strachov,
26 February 1869, in *Letters of Fyodor Michailovitch Dostoevsky
to his Family and Friends*, trans. Ethel Colburn Mayne (1914)

010902.ff.36

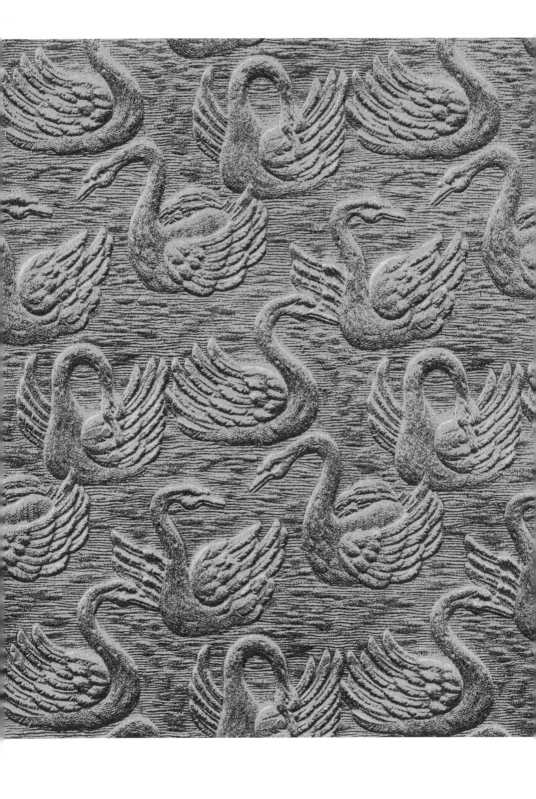

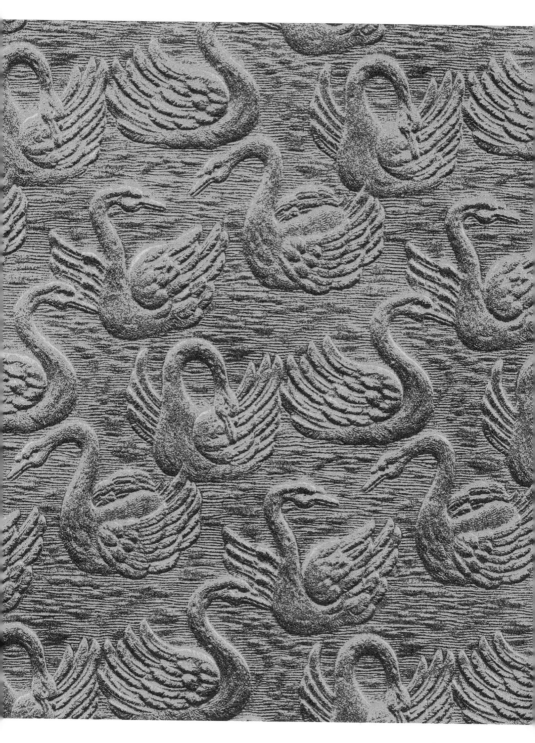

APRIL

❧ 1 April ❧

My Unripe Musings

Silent companions of the lonely hour,
    Friends, how can never alter or forsake,
Who for inconstant roving have no power,
    And all neglect, perforce, must calmly take, –
Let me return to you; this turmoil ending
    Which worldly cares have in my spirit wrought,
And, o'er your old familiar pages bending,
    Refresh my mind with many a tranquil thought:
Till, haply meeting there, from time to time,
    Fancies, the audible echo of my own,
'Twill be like hearing in a foreign clime
    My native language spoke in friendly tone,
And with a sort of welcome I shall dwell
On these, my unripe musings, told so well.

Caroline Norton, 'To My Books',
in *The Dream, and Other Poems* (1840)

1347.f.24

❧ 2 April ❧

A Sprig of Bays

Say, Britain, cou'd you ever boast,
Three Poets in an Age at most?
Our chilling Climate hardly bears
A Sprig of Bays in Fifty Years.

Jonathan Swift, *On Poetry; a Rhapsody* (1733)
11630.h.37

❧ 3 April ❧

Utterly Unsaleable and Absolutely Unread

The poets of our day have a glorious prospect before them,
if they will pursue their own interests through the wants of
the age, and write in prose. I should have written few verses
if, before I had acquired the bad habit of rhyming, I had
been honest enough to confess to myself that my thoughts
were not good enough for prose. The best poetry of that
age – the only poetry that is read – is written in prose,
and to be found in the prose of Scott, Dickens, Richter,
Thomas Carlyle, and others. Verse is a trick which the age
has seen through and despises. It is utterly unsaleable, and
absolutely unread.

Ebenezer Elliott, letter to Ebenezer Hingston,
14 November 1843, in *Life, Poetry and Letters of Ebenezer Elliott,
the Corn-Law Rhymer*, ed. John Watkins (1850)
10855.bb.24

❧ 4 April ❧

The Serial Enigma of the Dark

Conclusion of the book, ultimate: Evil is even, truth is an odd number and death a full stop. When a dog barks late at night and then retires again to bed, he punctuates and gives majesty to the serial enigma of the dark, laying it more evenly and heavily upon the fabric of the mind. Sweeney in the trees hears the sad baying as he sits listening on the branch, a huddle between the earth and heaven; and he hears also the answering mastiff that is counting the watches in the next parish. Bark answers bark till the call spreads like fire through all Erin. Soon the moon comes forth from behind her curtains riding full tilt across the sky, light-some and unperturbed in her immemorial calm. The eyes of the mad king upon the branch are upturned, whiter eyeballs in a white face, upturned in fear and supplication. His mind is but a shell.

Flann O'Brien, *At Swim-Two-Birds* (1939)

12632.A.15

✿ 5 April ✿

Your *Share of Beauty*

Those who live in towns should carefully remember this, for their own sakes, for their wives' sakes, for their children's sakes. Never lose an opportunity of seeing anything beautiful. Beauty is God's hand-writing – a wayside sacrament; welcome it in every fair face, every fair sky, every fair flower, and thank Him for it, the fountain of all loveliness, and drink it in, simply and earnestly, with all your eyes; it is a charmed draught, a cup of blessing.

Therefore I said that picture-galleries should be the townsman's paradise of refreshment. Of course, if he can get the real air, the real trees, even for an hour, let him take it, in God's name; but how many a man who cannot spare time for a daily country walk, may well slip into the National Gallery in Trafalgar Square (or the South Kensington Museum), or any other collection of pictures, for ten minutes. That garden, at least, flowers as gaily in winter as in summer. Those noble faces on the wall are never disfigured by grief or passion. There, in the space of a single room, the townsman may take his country walk – a walk beneath mountain peaks, blushing sunsets, with broad woodlands spreading out below it; a walk through green meadows, under cool mellow shades, and overhanging rocks, by rushing brooks, where he watches and watches till he seems to hear the foam whisper and to see the fishes leap; and his hard-worn heart wanders out free, beyond the grim city-world of stone and iron, smoky chimneys, and roaring wheels, into the world of beautiful things – the world which shall be hereafter – ay, which shall be! Believe it, toil-worn worker, in spite of thy foul alley, thy crowded lodging, thy grimed clothing, thy ill-fed children, thy thin, pale wife – believe it, thou too and thine, will some day have your share of beauty.

Charles Kingsley, 'Picture Galleries',
in *True Words for Brave Men* (1848)
4466.aa.8

 6 April

Dim Awaking

In looking at objects of Nature while I am thinking, as at
yonder moon dim-glimmering thro' the dewy window-pane,
I seem rather to be seeking, as it were asking, a symbolical
language for something within me that already and forever
exists, than observing anything new. Even when that latter
is the case, yet still I have always an obscure feeling as if
that new phenomenon were the dim Awaking of a forgotten
or hidden truth of my inner nature.

Samuel Taylor Coleridge, in *Anima Poetae: From the
Unpublished Note-books of Samuel Taylor Coleridge*,
ed. Ernest Hartley Coleridge (1895)

012356.ff.4

 7 April

I See the Moon

I see the moon,
And the moon sees me;
God bless the moon,
And God bless me.

*Gammer Gurton's Garland, or, The nursery Parnassus: a choice
collection of pretty songs and verses for the amusement of all little
good children who can neither read nor run (1784; repr. 1866)*

❧ 8 April ❧

Hypotheses and Hypotheses

You may have hypotheses and hypotheses. A man may say, if he likes, that the moon is made of green cheese: that is an hypothesis. But another man, who had devoted a great deal of time and attention to the subject, and availed himself of the most powerful telescopes and the results of the observations of others, declares that in his opinion it is probably composed of materials very similar to those of which our own earth is made up: and that is also an hypothesis. But I need not tell you that there is an enormous difference in the value of the two hypotheses. The one which is based on sound scientific knowledge is sure to have a corresponding value; and that which is a mere hasty random guess is likely to have but little value.

Thomas H. Huxley, *Darwiniana* (1902)
W 47 1563

❧ 9 April ❧

Facts are Like Cows

She always says, my lord, that facts are like cows. If you look them in the face hard enough they generally run away.

Dorothy L. Sayers, *Clouds of Witness* (1926)
XX.11426

❧ 10 April ❧

A Judicious Observer

A good ornithologist should be able to distinguish birds by their air as well as by their colours and shape; on the ground as well as on the wing, and in the bush as well as in the hand. For, though it must not be said that every species of birds has a manner peculiar to itself, yet there is somewhat, in most genera at least, that at first sight discriminates them and enables a judicious observer to pronounce upon them with some certainty.

Gilbert White, *The Natural History and Antiquities of Selborne, in the county of Southampton: with engravings and an appendix* (1789)

458.c.16

❧ 11 April ❧

What Learning is Called Sound

The Principle of Sound Learning is that the noise of vulgar fame should never trouble the cloistered calm of academic existence. Hence, learning is called sound when no one has ever heard of it; and 'sound scholar' is a term of praise applied to one another by learned men who have no reputation outside the University, and a rather queer one inside it. If you should write a book (you had better not), be sure that it is unreadable; otherwise you will be called 'brilliant' and forfeit all respect.

F. M. Cornford,
Microcosmographia Academia (1908)

RB.23.a.34427

❧ 12 April ❧

Tulip Beds and Cabbage Patches

Oh, my friends! You ask why the torrent of genius so rarely pours forth, so rarely floods and thunders and overwhelms your astonished soul? – Because, dear friends, on either bank dwell the cool, respectable gentlemen, whose summerhouses, tulip beds and cabbage patches would all be washed away, and who are therefore highly skilled in averting future dangers in good time, by damming and digging channels.

Johann Wolfgang von Goethe, *The Sorrows of Young Werther*
[1774], trans. Michael Hulse (2006)

ELD.DS.193273

❧ 13 April ❧

The Intermittency of Genius

One problem absorbs me above all others: it is what I will call the intermittency of genius. Why, more often than not, does a poet blossom out in his adolescence and early manhood, and then wither to pedantry and dullness?

Herbert Read,
Form in Modern Poetry (1932)
11867.bb.42

❧ 14 April ❧

A Bric-a-Brac Shop

It is a sad thing to think of, but there is no doubt that
Genius lasts longer than Beauty. That accounts for the fact
that we all take such pains to over-educate ourselves. In the
wild struggle for existence, we want to have something that
endures, and so we fill our minds with rubbish and facts,
in the silly hope of keeping our place. The thoroughly well-
informed man – that is the modern ideal. And the mind
of the thoroughly well-informed man is a dreadful thing.
It is like a bric-a-brac shop, all monsters and dust, with
everything priced above its proper value.

Oscar Wilde, *The Picture of Dorian Gray* (1890);
unauthorised ed.

X900/986

❧ 15 April ❧

To Be Beforehand with Oblivion

If it happens to the world to succeed in forgetting man or
woman, there is always some one at hand with a reminder
and a protest; even as the gloves we meant to lose reappear,
unwelcome, on our dressing-table. Sometimes the person
with the importunate memory makes so much haste and is

so nimble as even to be beforehand with oblivion; he will not wait for the death of a reputation before certifying – not the death, but the return to life. One uses, by the way, the words death and life, but there are a great many reputations for which these are words too large.

Alice Meynell, 'The Praises of Ouida' (1895),
repr. as 'Oblivion', in *The Wares of Autolycus: Selected Literary
Essays*, ed. P. M. Fraser (1965)

X.909/5804

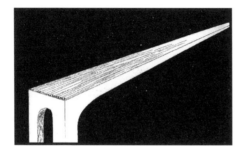

🦢 16 April 🦢

The Eternal Unity

Genius studies the casual thought, and far back in the womb of things sees the rays parting from one orb, that diverge, ere they fall, by infinite diameters. Genius watches the monad through all his masks as he performs the metempsychosis of nature. Genius detects through the fly, through the caterpillar, through the grub, through the egg, the constant individual; through countless individuals the fixed species; through many species the genus; through all genera the steadfast type; through all the kingdoms of organised life the eternal unity.

Ralph Waldo Emerson, 'History', in *Essays* (1841)

C.60.f.16

❧ 17 April ❧

A Little Wrong

The wisest and most dispassionate man in existence, merely wishing to go from one stile in a field to the opposite, will not walk quite straight – he is always going a little wrong, and always correcting himself; and I can only congratulate the individualist who is able to say that his general course of life has been of a less undulating character.

Thomas H. Huxley, 'The Struggle for Existence: A Programme' (1888), in *Evolution and Ethics, and Other Essays* (1906)
W12/9085

❧ 18 April ❧

The Fur that Warms

The fur that warms a monarch, warm'd a bear.

Alexander Pope, *An Essay on Man... Epistle IV* (1734)
12273.m.1.(3.)

❧ 19 April ❧

Pain to the Bear

The Puritan hated bear-baiting, not because it gave pain to the bear, but because it gave pleasure to the spectators.

Thomas Babington Macaulay,
The History of England, vol.1 (1849)
9525.c.8

❦ 20 April ❦

Bear-like

This sixth and possibly final volume of *Ego* – I can feel an October nip in the air – will be my thirty-seventh book, unless, of course, I publish some more while it is writing. This means thirty-seven slabs of stolen time. Every moment spent on *Ego* had been filched from the hours I should have been giving to this editor or that. George Meredith relinquished his job as publisher's reader because he could live by his novels. But since, all deductions made, my books have never brought me in even a hundred pounds a year, I must continue reviewing plays, films, novels. And then there is the old income-tax nuisance. My arrears tie me to the stake. Bear-like, I must fight the course.

James Agate, diary entry, Monday 3 August 1942, in
Ego 6: Once More the Autobiography of James Agate (1944)

10860.aaa.30

❦ 21 April ❦

Words Freeze in Your Mouth

On Mount Etna the words freeze in your mouth and you may make ice of them.

Just as iron rusts unless it is used, and water purifies or, in cold, turns to ice, so our intellect spoils unless it is kept in use.

You do ill if you praise, and still worse if you reprove in a matter you do not understand.

When Fortune comes, seize her in front with a sure hand, because behind she is bald.

Leonardo da Vinci, *The Notebooks of Leonardo da Vinci*, ed. Jean Paul Richter, vol.II (1883; 1970 edn) q73/14828 Vol.I

❦ 22 April ❦

The Most Miraculous of All Things

Certainly the Art of Writing is the most miraculous of all things man has devised. Odin's *Runes* were the first form of the work of a Hero; Books written words, are still miraculous *Runes*, the latest form! In Books lies the *soul* of the whole Past Time; the articulate audible voice of the Past, when the body and material substance of it has altogether vanished like a dream. Mighty fleets and armies, harbors and arsenals, vast cities, high-domed, many-engined – they are precious, great: but what do they become? Agamemnon, the many Agamemnons, Pericleses, and their Greece; all is gone now to some ruined fragments, dumb mournful wrecks and blocks: but the Books of Greece! There Greece, to every thinker, still very literally lives: can be called up again into life. No magic *Rune* is stranger than a Book. All that Mankind has done, thought, gained or been: it is lying as in magic preservation in the pages of Books. They are the chosen possession of men.

Thomas Carlyle, from *On Heroes, Hero Worship,*
& the Heroic in History (1841)

722.g.20

🦢

🦢 23 April 🦢

What You Can Make It Do

It is difficult even to talk about plastics, because they constitute such a wide range of materials with an even wider range of properties. Even a particular plastic resin can offer different sorts of strength, moisture protection, flexibility, and appearance, depending on how it is processed ... While most people have a vague idea that plastics are very complicated strings of molecules, an emotional grasp of "what they really are" is elusive. Unlike wood or paper or even steel, plastics don't have character, but, rather, multiple personalities. The right question to ask about a plastic is not what it is, but what you can make it do.

Thomas Hine, *The Total Package: the evolution and secret*
meanings of boxes, bottles, cans and tubes (1995)

YC.1996.b.2463

24 April

You Are Likely to End With

Describe an individual and you may end with a type; describe
a type and you are likely to end with – nothing.

F. Scott Fitzgerald, 'The Rich Boy',
in *All the Sad Young Men* (1926)
12710.b.3

25 April

All Melted Together

If we choose to let our conjecture run wild, then animals, our
fellow brethren in pain, disease, death, suffering and famine
– our salves in the most laborious works, our companions in
our amusements – they may partake [of?] our origin in one
common ancestor – we may be all melted together.

Charles Darwin, notebook, 1837,
q. in *Life and Letters of Charles Darwin*,
ed. Francis Darwin (1887)
10859.g.27

🦢 26 April 🦢

A Pattern Called a War

I shall go
Up and down,
In my gown.
Gorgeously arrayed,
Boned and stayed.
And the softness of my body will be guarded from embrace
By each button, hook, and lace.
For the man who should loose me is dead,
Fighting with the Duke in Flanders,
In a pattern called a war.
Christ! What are patterns for?

Amy Lowell, from 'Patterns', in
Selected Poems of Amy Lowell, ed. John Livingston Lowes (1928)
11689.b.14

27 April

The Little Creature of his Culture

The life-history of the individual is first and foremost an accommodation to the patterns and standards traditionally handed down in his community. From the moment of his birth the customs into which he is born shapes his experience and behavior. By the time he can talk, he is the little creature of his culture, and by the time he is grown and able to take part in its activities, its habits are his habits, its beliefs his beliefs, its impossibilities his impossibilities.

Ruth Benedict,
Patterns of Culture (1934; 1989 edn)
93/06598

28 April

Des Anders Denkenden

Freiheit is immer nur Freiheit des anders Denkenden.

(Freedom is always and exclusively freedom for those who think differently.)

Rosa Luxemburg,
Die Russische Revolution (1922)
W14/8447

❧ 29 April ❧

The Militancy of Women

The militancy of men, through all the centuries, has drenched the world with blood, and for these deeds of horror and destruction men have been rewarded with monuments, with great songs and epics. The militancy of women has harmed no human life save the lives of those who fought the battle of righteousness. Time alone will reveal what reward will be allotted to the women.

This we know, that in the black hour that has just struck Europe, the men are turning to their women and calling on them to make up the work of keeping civilisation alive. Through all the harvest fields, in orchards and vineyards, women are garnering food for those even who fight, as well as for the children left fatherless by war. In the cities the women are keeping open the shops, they are driving trucks and trams, and are altogether attending to a multitude of business. [...] So ends, for the present, the war of women against men. As of old, the women become the nurturing mothers of men, their sisters and uncomplaining helpmates. The future lies far ahead [...] but the struggle for the full enfranchisement of women has not been abandoned; it has simply, for the moment, been placed in abeyance. When the clash of arms ceases, when normal, peaceful, rational society resumes its functions, the demand will again be made. If it is not quickly granted, then once more the women will take up the arms they to-day generously lay down. There can be no real peace in the world until woman, the mother half of the human family, is given liberty in the councils of the world.

Emmeline Pankhurst, *My Own Story* (1914)

08416.k.49

30 April

The Nobodies!

Heroes accomplish much brilliant butchery; they are great dust-raisers and provokers of tumult; they find employment for the players on brazen instruments, and the perpetrators of heroic verse; but there are precious few of them in history who do not fill places that would have been better filled if they had left them vacant. [...] Music, and the arts, and the richest treasures of tradition, romance and fairy lore, as well as most of the handicrafts, and much of the useful kind of learning, are less due to the labours of the heroes than to the slow accumulation of the added mites of long generations of Nobodies. [...] Who does all the loading and firing, the charging and cheering, on the battlefield? The Nobodies! Who defended the pass at Thermopylae, and the biscuit-box breastwork at Rorke's Drift? The Nobodies! Who invented needles, and files, and umbrellas, and meerschaum pipes, and soap, and blotting pads, and beefsteak puddings, and the Greek mythology, and warming pans, and double stout, and lucifer matches, and the Norse Edda, and kippered herrings, and kissing, and divided skirts, and the Union Jack of Old England, and *The Clarion*? The Nobodies!

Who wrote Shakespeare's plays –! [...] Of what stuff do our novelists, poets, orators, and painters weave their spells? Of the loves and trials, the smiles and tears, the follies and the heroisms of the Nobodies.

Robert Blatchford, *The Numquam Papers* (1891)

1608/4528

MAY

❄ 1 May ❀

The Autobiography of Pickpockets

The classics of the *papier maché* age of our drama have taken up the salutary belief that England expects every driveller to do his Memorabilia. Modern primer-makers must needs leave *confessions* behind them, as if they were so many Rousseaus. Our weakest mob-orators think it is a hard case if they cannot spout to posterity. Cabin-boys and drummers are busy with their commentaries *de bello Gallico*; the John Gilpins of 'the nineteenth century' are the historians of their own *anabases*; and, thanks to 'the march of the intellect', we are already rich in the autobiography of pickpockets.

John Gibson Lockhart, review of ten works of autobiography, in *The Quarterly Review*, vol.XXXV, January–March 1827

Crawford 1865.(1.)

❧ 2 May ❧

We're So Very, Very Low

We plough and sow – we're so very, very low
    That we delve in the dirty clay,
Till we bless the plain – with the golden grain,
    And the vale with the fragrant hay.
Our place we know, – we're so very low,
    'Tis down at the landlord's feet:
We're not too low – the bread to grow,
    But too low the bread to eat.

[...]

We're low – we're low – mere rabble, we know,
    But at our plastic power,
The mould at the lordling's feet will grow
    Into palace and church and tower.
Then prostrate fall – in the rich man's hall,
    And cringe at the rich man's door;
We're not too low to build the wall,
    But too low to tread the floor.

Ernest Jones, 'The Song of the Lower Classes',
in *Modern Street Ballads*, ed. John Ashton (1888)

11601.f.29

❧ 3 May ❦

The Devices

Ernest Jones, in the second year of his imprisonment, was so broken in health, that he could no longer stand upright – he was found lying on the floor of his cell, and then, only, taken to the prison hospital. He was told that if he would petition for his release and promise to abjure politics for the future, the remainder of his sentence would be remitted – but he refused his liberty on those conditions, said the work he had once begun he would never turn from, and was accordingly reconsigned to his cell. [...] During his imprisonment, and before pen, ink and paper were allowed, he wrote some of the finest poems in the English language. The devices by which he obtained writing materials were amusing. Pens he got by finding occasionally a feather from a rook's wing that had dropped in the prison yard. This quill he cut secretly with a razor, when brought to him twice a week to shave; an ink bottle he contrived to make from a piece of soap he got from the washingshed, and this he filled with ink from the ink bottle when he was allowed to write his quarterly letters, the fly-leaves of a Bible, prayer-book, and of any books he was, as before stated allowed to read. But one poem – The New World – was composed before he had succeeded in securing ink, and this was written almost entirely with his own blood.

James Crossley,
Ernest Jones: Who is he? What has he done? (1857?)

W55/3126

❧ 4 May ❀

Blood-Letting

In former times, when the barber united with his art that of surgery, or at least of blood-letting, the barber's-pole had a real significance. The gilt ball at the top represented the brass basin used for lathering the customers; the pole represented the staff held by persons during venesection; while the two spiral ribbons painted on the pole represented, – the one, the bandage twisted round the arm previous to blood-letting, and the other, the bandage used for binding up the arm afterwards.

William Henry P. Phyfe,
5000 Facts and Fancies: A Cyclopaedia of Important, Curious, Quaint and Unique Information in History; Literature, Science, Art and Nature Including Noteworthy Historical Events; Civil, Military and Religious Institutions; Scientific Facts and Theories; Natural Curiosities; Famous Buildings, Monuments, Statues, Paintings, and Other Works of Art and Utility; Celebrated Literary Productions; Sobriquets and Nicknames; Literary Pseudonyms; Mythological and Imaginary Characters; Political and Slang Terms; Derivations of Peculiar Words and Phrases; Etc., Etc. (1901)

12220.c.5

❧ 5 May ❧

The Cultivator of Beards

We might write a treatise on beards. We might show how shaving is primarily, and in its origins, a sign of penitence and voluntary celibacy – how the fashion of shaving among men who are neither penitent nor celibate derives from puritan notions of the vanity of male display (hence its universality in our puritan-industrial civilization) – how shaving is naturally approved of by women; for women, as Chaucer's Wife of Bath was at great pains to show, desire nothing more than power over their husbands – how the word 'barber' means cultivator of beards and not him who cuts them off – be we refrain. It is sufficient if we simply point out that the beard is the proper clothing of the male chin, and the all-sufficing garment of differentiation.

Eric Gill, *Clothes* (1931)

W9/0332

❖ 6 May ❖

The Records of Velim

In the outward beauty, These be the Records of velim, these be the parchmins, the endictments, and the evidences that shall condemn many of us, at the last day, our *own skins*; we have the book of God, the Law, written in our own hearts; we have the image of God imprinted in our own souls; wee have the character, and seal of God stamped in us, in our baptism; and, all this is bound up in this velim, in this parchmin, in this skin of ours, and we neglect book, and image, and character, and seal, and all for the covering.

John Donne, *The second volume preached by that learned and revered divine, John Donne* (1649)

C.122.i.2

❧ 7 May ❧

Associations Arise

In circumcision, God subjugates men in a form of 'writing'
or accounting or numbering, and writing as numbering
was almost as important a sign of possession and control
as naming. Circumcision is the earliest form of God's
'writing' the male body into a book of men chosen, sealed,
and confirmed for his exclusive and unique theocratic
community, and this phallic sign 'shall be in your flesh for
an everlasting covenant' (Gen.17.13). [...] As often happens
in biblical and early modern narrative, associations arise
between the human genitals and the human heart, and we
shall see in the prophetic writing and in the New Testament
a special emphasis on the 'circumcision of the heart'.

Robert A. Erickson,
The Language of the Heart, 1600–1750 (1997)
YC.1998.b.5173

❋ 8 May ❋

The Familiar Hallucinations of the Insane

A common form of vision is a phantasmagoria, or the appearance of a crowd of phantoms, perhaps hurrying past like men in a street. It is occasionally seen in broad daylight, much more often in the dark; it may be at the instant of putting out the candle, but it generally comes on when the person is in bed, preparing to sleep, but is by no means yet asleep. I know no less than three men, eminent in the scientific world, who have these phantasmagoria in one form or another. A near relative of my own had them in a marked degree. She was eminently sane, and of such good constitution that her faculties were hardly impaired until near her death at ninety. She frequently described them to me. It gave her amusement during an idle hour to watch these faces, for their expression was always pleasing, though never strikingly so. No two faces were ever alike, and they never resembled that of any acquaintance. When she was not well the faces usually came nearer to her, sometimes almost suffocatingly close. She never mistook them for reality, although they were very distinct. This is quite a typical case, similar in most respects to many others that I have.

A notable proportion of sane persons have had not only visions, but actual hallucinations of sight, sound, or other sense, at one or more periods of their lives. I have a considerable packet of instances contributed by my personal friends, besides a large number communicated to me by other correspondents. [...] In short, the familiar hallucinations of the insane are to be met with far more frequently than is commonly supposed, among people moving in society and in normal health.

Francis Galton,
Inquiries into Human Faculty and Its Development (1883)
W47/1769

❋ 9 May ❋

A Peculiar, Little-Known Disease Process

On the whole, it is evident that we are dealing with a
peculiar, little-known disease process. In recent years
these particular disease-processes have been detected in
great numbers. This fact should stimulate us to further
study and analysis of this particular disease. We must not
be satisfied to force it into the existing group of well-known
disease patterns. It is clear that there exist many more
mental diseases than our text books indicate. In many such
cases, a further histological examination must be effected
to determine the characteristics of each single case. We
must reach the stage in which the vast well-known disease
groups must be subdivided into many smaller groups, each
one with its own clinical and anatomical characteristics.

Alois Alzheimer, 'A Characteristic Disease of the Cerebral
Cortex' (1906), in *The Early Story of Alzheimer's Disease*,
eds Katherine Bick, Luigi Amaducci, Giancarlo Pepeu (1987)

88/09675

❧ 10 May ❧

No Process of Proof but Deduction

These sciences have no principles besides definitions and axioms, and no process of proof but *deduction*; this process, however, assuming a most remarkable character; and exhibiting a combination of simplicity and complexity, of rigour and generality, quite unparalleled in other subjects.

William Whewell, *The Philosophy of the Inductive Sciences, Founded Upon Their History* (1840)

536.h.23

❧ ❧

❧ 11 May ❧

The Creative Source of Discovery

Imagination, as well as reason, is necessary to perfection in the philosophical mind. A rapidity of combination, a power of perceiving analogies, and of comparing them by facts, in the creative source of discovery. Discrimination and delicacy of sensation, so important in physical research, are other words for taste; and the love of nature is the same passion, as the love of the magnificent, the sublime and the beautiful.

[Humphrey Davy], 'Parallels between Art and Science', in *The Director: A Literary and Scientific Journal*, ed. T. F. Dibdin (1807)

P.P.5464

❧ 12 May ❧

The Parts of My Brain Now Atrophied

My mind seems to have become a kind of machine for grinding general laws out of large collections of facts, but why this should have caused the atrophy of that part of the brain alone, on which the higher tastes depend, I cannot conceive. A man with a mind more highly organised or better constituted than mine, would not, I suppose, have thus suffered; and if I had to live my life again, I would have made a rule to read some poetry and listen to some music at least once every week; for perhaps the parts of my brain now atrophied would thus have been kept active through use. The loss of these tastes is a loss of happiness, and may possibly be injurious to the intellect, and more probably to the moral character, by enfeebling the emotional part of our nature.

Charles Darwin, *The Life and Letters of Charles Darwin,
Including an autobiographical chapter,*
vol.1, ed. Francis Darwin (1887)

10859.g.27

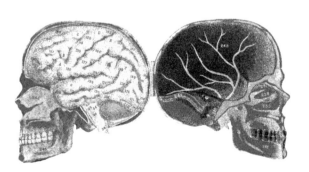

❧ 13 May ❧

The Inmost Essence of Truth

I have my own idea about art, and it is this: What most people regard as fantastic and lacking in universality, I hold to be the inmost essence of truth. Arid observation of everyday trivialities I have long since ceased to regard as realism – it is quite the reverse. In any newspaper one takes up, one comes across reports of wholly authentic facts, which nevertheless strike one as extraordinary. Our writers regard them as fantastic, and take no account of them; and yet they are the truth, for they are facts. But who troubles to observe, record, describe them? They happen every day and every moment, therefore they are not 'exceptional' ...

Fyodor Dostoevsky, letter to Nikolay Strachov,
26 February 1869, in *Letters of Fyodor M. Dostoevsky*,
trans. Ethel Colburn Mayne (1914)

010902.ff.36

❧ ❧

❧ 14 May ❧

The Supposed Fact

Our religion has materialised itself in the fact, in the supposed fact; it has attached its emotion to the fact, and now the fact is failing it [...] More and more we will discover that we have to turn to poetry to interpret life for us, to console us, to sustain us.

Matthew Arnold, 'The Study of Poetry',
in *Essays in Criticism: Second Series* (1888)

11850.p.25

❦ 15 May ❦

Unintermittent Skepticism

It is through a conviction of the inadequacy of all formulas to cover the facts of nature, it is by a constant recollection of the fallibility of the best instructed intelligence, and by an unintermittent skepticism which goes out of its way to look for difficulties, that scientific progress has been made possible.

James Anthony Froude,
Short Studies on Great Subjects, vol.II (1896)
W46/8336

❦ 16 May ❦

Limited Dimensionality

Yet I exist in the hope that these memoirs, in some manner, I know not how, may find their way to the minds of humanity in Some Dimension, and may stir up a race of rebels who shall refuse to be confined to limited Dimensionality.

A. Square [Edwin A. Abbot],
Flatland: A Romance of Many Dimensions (1884)
YC.2000.a.3781

※ 17 May ❁

Is it Those Three-Cornered Things?

MISS SUSAN: What is algebra exactly; is it those three-cornered things?
PHOEBE: It is x minus y equals z plus y and things like that. And all the time you are saying they are equal, you feel in your heart, why should they be?

J. M. Barrie, *The Plays of J. M. Barrie: Quality Street: A Comedy* (1925)

W 69/4554

※ 18 May ❁

A Certain Very Small Gland

But, after careful examination, it seems to me quite evident that the part of the body in which the soul immediately exercises its functions is neither the heart, nor even the brain as a whole, but solely the most interior part of it, which is a certain very small gland, situated in the middle of its substance, and so suspended above the passage by which the spirits of its anterior cavities communicate with those of the posterior, that the slightest motions in it may greatly affect the course of these spirits, and, reciprocally, that the slightest changes which take place in the course of the spirits may greatly affect the motions of this gland.

René Descartes, *Passions of the Soul* (1649), trans. Stephen Voss (1989)

YD.2013.a.337

❋ 19 May ❋

Completely Unimportant

'It is completely unimportant,' said Poirot. 'That is why it is so interesting,' he added softly.

Agatha Christie,
The Murder of Roger Ackroyd (1926)
Cup.410.f.554

❋ 20 May ❋

The Last Vestiges

We have often expressed a wish that our various dialects might be rescued from oblivion, while yet in existence. Even at this moment they are gradually vanishing; and, unless the last vestiges be speedily caught, it will be in vain to seek for them hereafter.

Samuel Pegge, *Anecdotes of the English Language:
chiefly regarding the local dialect of London and its Environs* (1814)
W3/5579

✤ 21 May ✤

To Get One's Irish Up

Get one's Irish up – to become determined in one's purpose.

Maurice H. Weseen, *A Dictionary of American Slang* (1935)

12983.s.9

✤ 22 May ✤

Romantic Ireland

Romantic Ireland's dead and gone.
It's with O'Leary in the grave.

W. B. Yeats, from 'September 13', first published as 'Romance
in Ireland' 1913, in *Responsibilities: Poems and a Play* (1914)

Cup.510.ad.20

❧ 23 May ❧

The Fatuity of Idiots

The moment the very name of Ireland is mentioned, the English seem to bid adieu to common feeling, common prudence and common sense, and to act with the barbarity of tyrants and the fatuity of idiots.

Sydney Smith, *Peter Plymley's Letters, and Selected Essays* no.2, 1807 (1886)

12208.bb.15/64

❧❧

❧ 24 May ❧

Grasping, Grinding Tyranny

I know of nothing better calculated to make the blood boil than the cold accounts of the grasping, grinding tyranny to which the Irish people have been subjected, and to which, and not to any inability of the land to support its inhabitants, Irish pauperism and Irish famine are to be attributed; and were it not for the enervating effect which the history of the world proves to be everywhere the result of abject poverty, it would be difficult to resist something like a feeling of contempt for a race who, stung by such wrongs, have only occasionally murdered a landlord!

Henry George, *Progress and Poverty: An Inquiry into the Cause of Industrial Depressions, and of Increase of Want with Increase of Wealth: the Remedy* (1879; 1953 edn)

W73/7593

❀ 25 May ❀

Being Robbed

Tuesday 23 December

I will make this hasty note about being robbed. I put my bag under my coat at Marshall & Snelgrove's. I turned; & felt, before I looked 'It is gone'. So it was. Then began questions & futile messages. Then the detective came. He stopped a respectable elderly woman apparently shopping. They exchanged remarks about 'the usual one – no she's not here today. It's a young woman in brown fur.' Meanwhile I was ravaged, of course, with my own futile wishes – how I had thought, as I put down my bag, this is foolish. I was admitted to the underworld. I imagined the brown young woman peeping, pouncing. And it was gone my 6 pounds - my two brooches – all because of that moment. They throw the bags away, said the detective. These dreadful women come here – but not so much as to some of the Oxford St. shops. Fluster, regret, humiliation, curiosity, something frustrated, foolish, something jarred, by this underworld – a foggy evening – going home, penniless – thinking of my green bag – imagining the woman rifling it – her home – her husband – Now to Rodmell in the fog.

Virginia Woolf, *The Diary of Virginia Woolf, 1925–1930* (1980)
80/9684 vol 3

❁ 26 May ❁

A Queer Adventure

Xmas Day

Dearest Dolphin

I rang you up on Tuesday, but you were out. It was only to say that that we sent you a black coat; and that if you hate, it, or if it doesn't fit, you can change it. I thought it might come in useful in the evening; anyhow keep you warm in the country.

... I had a queer adventure by the way, the day I got your coat at Marshall and Snelgroves. I was given £6 to buy Xmas presents; I put my bag under my moleskin, and turned, for one moment, to try on your coat. Then I thought I ought not to leave the bag, so turned to get it – and behold – in that second a thief had snatched it! There was then a great hue and cry, and a detective appeared, and they said a woman in brown fur had been seen; but of course they could not catch her; so there I was, penniless, without key, spectacles, cigarette case or handkerchief. Marshall's refused to lend me a penny as they said I was not on their books; but the detective gave me 10/- of his own. Later that night the bag was found, thrown in a drain; and marvellously, though the £6 were gone, the thief had left my spectacles, keys, and one gold earring. I had just bought two for a present. So didn't do as badly as I might.

Virginia Woolf, *A Reflection of the Other Person: The Letters of Virginia Woolf 1929–31* (1978)

78/29798

❧ 27 May ❧

A Kind of Intellectual Cowardice

There is often to be found in men devoted to literature a kind of intellectual cowardice, which, whoever converses much among them, may observe frequently to depress the alacrity of enterprise, and, by consequence, to retard the improvement of science. They have annexed to every species of knowledge some chimerical character of terrour and inhibition, which they transmit, without much reflection, from one to another; they first fright themselves, and then propagate the panick to their scholars and acquaintance. One study is inconsistent with a lively imagination, another with a solid judgment: one is improper in the early parts of life, another requires so much time, that it is not to be attempted at an advanced age; one is dry and contracts the sentiments, another is diffuse and overburdens the memory; one is insufferable to taste and delicacy, and another wears out life in the study of words, and is useless to a wise man, who desires only the knowledge of things.

Samuel Johnson, *The Rambler* no.25, 12 June 1750

RB.23.a.8163

❧ 28 May ❧

A Chartered Libertine

I have always been from my very incapacity of methodical
writing a chartered libertine free to worship & free to rail
lucky when I was understood but never esteemed near
enough to the institutions & mind of society to deserve
the notice of the masters of literature & religion. I have
appreciated fully the advantage of my position for I well
know that there was no scholar less willing or less able to be
a polemic. I could not give account of myself if challenged I
could not possibly give you one of the 'arguments' on which
as you cruelly hint any position of mine stands. For I do not
know, I confess, what arguments mean in reference to any
expression of a thought.

Ralph Waldo Emerson, from a letter, 8 October 1838,
in *The Letters of Ralph Waldo Emerson*, vol.II,
ed. Ralph L. Rusk (1939)

010921.p.11

❧❧

❧ 29 May ❧

We Can't Whistle It

What we can't say we can't say, and we can't whistle it either.

Frank Plumpton Ramsay, *The Foundations of Mathematics:
and other logical essays* (1931; 1965 edn)

08460.g.1/61

❦ 30 May ❦

The Fire Was Within Myself

All at once, without warning of any kind, I found myself wrapped in a flame-colored cloud. For an instant I thought of fire, an immense conflagration somewhere close by in that great city; the next, I knew that the fire was within myself. Directly afterward there came upon me a sense of exultation, of immense joyousness accompanied or immediately followed by an intellectual illumination impossible to describe. Among other things, I did not merely come to believe, but I saw that the universe is not composed of dead matter, but is, on the contrary, a living Presence; I became conscious in myself of eternal life. It was not a conviction that I would have eternal life, but a consciousness that I possessed eternal life then; I saw that all men are immortal; that the cosmic order is such that without any peradventure all things work together for the good of each and all; that the foundation principle of the world, of all the worlds, is what we call love, and that the happiness of each and all is in the long run absolutely certain. The vision lasted a few seconds and was gone; but the memory of it and the sense of the reality of what it taught has remained during the quarter of a century which has since elapsed.

Richard Maurice Bucke, *Cosmic Consciousness: A Study in the Evolution of the Human Mind* (1901; 1905 edn)

8465.i.10

❄ 31 May ❄

Which Way I Fly

Which way I fly is Hell; myself am Hell;
And, in the lowest deep, a lower deep
Still threatening to devour me opens wide,
To which the Hell I suffer seems a Heaven.

John Milton,
Paradise Lost [1667], ed. Alastair Fowler (1971)
X.0909/105.(7.)

JUNE

⤺ 1 June ⤻

My Naked Simple Life

My naked simple Life was I;
 That Act so strongly shin'd
Upon the earth, the sea, the sky,
It was the substance of my mind;
 The sense itself was I.
I felt no dross nor matter in my Soul,
No brims nor borders, such as in a bowl
We see. My essence was capacity,
 That felt all things;
 The thought that springs
Therefrom's itself. It hath no other wings
 To spread abroad, nor eyes to see,
  Nor hands distinct to feel,
   Nor knees to kneel.
But being simple like the Deity
 In its own centre is a sphere
  Not shut up here, but everywhere.

Thomas Traherne, 'My Spirit', in
The Poetical Works of Thomas Traherne,
ed. Bertram Dobell (1903)

11607.h.8

❮ 2 June ❯

Dedicated

DEDICATED TO MYSELF

Radclyffe Hall, dedication to *A Saturday Life* (1925)
NN.10636

❮ 3 June ❯

I Bequeath Myself

I celebrate myself, and sing myself,
And what I assume you shall assume,
For every atom belonging to me as good belongs to you.
[...]
I bequeath myself to the dirt to grow from the grass I love,
If you want me again look for me under your boot-soles.

You will hardly know who I am or what I mean,
But I shall be good health to you nevertheless,
And filter and fibre your blood.

Walt Whitman, from 'Song of Myself',
in *Leaves of Grass* (1855)
C.58.g.4

≪ 4 June ≫

With These Burthens On Him

It would have been no small thing, had he done no more than to support himself and his family during so many years by writing, without ever being in debt, or in any pecuniary difficulty; holding, as he did, opinions, both in politics and in religion, which were more odious to all persons of influence, and to the common run of prosperous Englishmen in that generation than either before or since; and being not only a man whom nothing would have induced to write against his convictions, but one who invariably threw into everything he wrote, as much of his convictions as he thought the circumstances would in any way permit: being, it must also be said, one who never did anything negligently; never undertook any task, literary or other, on which he did not conscientiously bestow all the labour necessary for performing it adequately. But he, with these burthens on him, planned, commenced, and completed, the History of India; and this in the course of about ten years, a shorter time than has been occupied (even by writers who had no other employment) in the production of almost any other historical work of equal bulk, and of anything approaching to the same amount of reading and research. And to this is to be added, that during the whole period, a considerable part of almost every day was employed in the instruction of his children: in the case of one of whom, myself, he exerted an amount of labour, care, and perseverance rarely, if ever, employed for a similar purpose, in endeavouring to give, according to his own conception, the highest order of intellectual education.

John Stuart Mill,
The Autobiography of John Stuart Mill (1873)
1609/5193

≪ 5 June ≫

Harsh Voices, Lethargic Attitudes, Neurotic Gestures

Certainly in the lesson in aesthetic appreciation the principle of the first impression is all-important, and the best advice that can be given to a teacher of appreciation is that he should lavish care and thought upon making the first impression which the child receives from a work of art a powerful impression, and that the greater the work of art, the greater the amount of care and thought he should lavish. [...] It is clear [...] that some teachers are not fitted to give these lessons. Harsh voices, lethargic attitudes, neurotic gestures, should not be associated with the pupil's first impression of a great work of art. [...] There is plenty of room in school for teachers fat as well as teachers lean, teachers with loud voices as well as teachers with soft voices, and various other forms of physical unfitness may be thrown into the background by genuine beauty of character. [...] But the principle remains: [...] care should be taken to exclude every unfavorable circumstance. As the minds of the pupils play in retrospect around the lesson, there should not come, if we can prevent it, a single harsh or discordant association, – no memory of a rasping voice, an unsympathetic face, a gloomy day, a crowded or an ugly classroom, or a morning hour broken by a dozen interruptions from the outside.

Frank Herbert Hayward, *The Lesson in Appreciation:*
An Essay on the Pedagogics of Beauty (1915)

X.529/2187.(1.)

≪ 6 June ≫

How to Strike the Balance

The real, if unavowed, purpose of fiction is to give pleasure by gratifying the love of the uncommon in human experience, mental or corporeal.

This is done all the more perfectly in proportion as the reader is alluded to believe the personages true and real like himself.

Solely to this latter end a work of fiction should be a precise transcript of ordinary life: but,

The uncommon would be absent and the interest lost, Hence,

The writer's problem is, how to strike the balance between the uncommon and the ordinary so as on the one hand to give interest, on the other to give reality.

Thomas Hardy, notebook entry July 1881,
from *The Early Life of Thomas Hardy, 1840–1891* (1928)

010855.f.35

≪ 7 June ≫

A Fragment of an Underdone Potato

'You don't believe in me,' observed the Ghost.
'I don't,' said Scrooge.
'What evidence would you have of my reality, beyond that of your senses?'
'I don't know,' said Scrooge.
'Why do you doubt your senses?'
'Because,' said Scrooge, 'a little thing affects them. A slight disorder of the stomach makes them cheats. You may be an undigested bit of beef, a blot of mustard, a crumb of cheese, a fragment of an underdone potato. There's more of gravy than of grave about you, whatever you are!'

Charles Dickens, *A Christmas Carol* (1843)

12275.aaa.2

≪ 8 June ≫

To Be Used with the Utmost Caution

The only supernatural agents which can in any manner be allowed to us moderns, are ghosts; but of these I would advise an author to be extremely sparing. These are indeed, like arsenic, and other dangerous drugs in physic, to be used with the utmost caution; nor would I advise the introduction of them at all in those works, or by those authors, to which, or to whom, a horse-laugh in the reader would be any great prejudice or mortification.

As for elves and fairies, and other such mummery, I purposely omit the mention of them, as I should be very unwilling to confine within any bounds those surprising imaginations, for whose vast capacity the limits of human nature are too narrow; whose works are to be considered as a new creation; and who have consequently just right to do what they will with their own.

Man, therefore, is the highest subject (unless on very extraordinary occasions indeed) which presents itself to the pen of our historian, or of our poet; and in relating his actions, great care is to be taken that we do not exceed the capacity of the agent we describe.

Henry Fielding,
The History of Tom Jones, a Foundling (1749)

1472.aa.28

❮ 9 June ❯

Books as Slaves Exposed Naked for Sale

I don't intend my books for the generality of readers. I count it a mistake of our mistaken democracy, that every man who can read print is allowed to believe that he can read all that is printed. I count it a misfortune that serious books are exposed in the public market, like slaves exposed naked for sale. But there we are, since we live in an age of mistaken democracy, we must go through with it.

D. H. Lawrence, *Fantasia of the Unconscious* (1923)
08465.df.5

❮ 10 June ❯

It is Only a Novel

Although our productions have afforded more extensive and unaffected pleasure than those of any other literary corporation in the world, no species of composition has been so much decried ... 'And what are you reading, Miss —?' 'Oh! it is only a novel!' replies the young lady; while she lays down her book with affected indifference, or momentary shame. 'It is only Cecilia, or Camilla, or Belinda': or, in short, only some work in which the greatest powers of the mind are displayed, in which the most thorough knowledge of human nature, the happiest delineation of its varieties, the liveliest effusions of wit and humour, are conveyed to the world in the best chosen language.

Jane Austen, *Northanger Abbey* (1818)
12600.e.2

≮ 11 June ≯

The Tides of the Mind

If life is not always poetical, it is at least metrical. Periodicity rules over the mental experience of man, according to the path of the orbit of his thoughts. Distances are not gauged, ellipses not measured, velocities not ascertained, times not known. Nevertheless, the recurrence is sure. What the mind suffered last week, or last year, it does not suffer now; but it will suffer again next week or next year. Happiness is not a matter of events; it depends upon the tides of the mind. Disease is metrical, closing in at shorter and shorter periods towards death, sweeping abroad at longer and longer intervals towards recovery. Sorrow for one cause was intolerable yesterday, and will be intolerable to-morrow; to-day it is easy to bear, but the cause has not passed. Even the burden of a spiritual distress unsolved bound to leave the heart to a temporary peace; and remorse itself does not remain – it returns. Gaiety takes us by a dear surprise. If we had made a course of notes of its visits, we might have been on the watch, and would have had an expectation instead of a discovery. No one makes such observations; in all the diaries of students of the interior world, there have never come to light the records of the Kepler of such cycles.

Alice Meynell, 'The Rhythm of Life',
in *The Rhythm of Life: And Other Essays* (1893)

012357.k.9

≪ 12 June ≫

Single Acts

People talk about repeated actions going habits (this is a very old thesis). But much more interesting to me is the curious effect on character which may be produced by single acts, seeming to raise the mind to a higher level, or to give a power previously unknown. I think that this is especially the case with acts of courage, or disinterestedness, or forgiveness.

Benjamin Jowett, letter to Lady Abercromby, 8 September 1882, in *The Life and Letters of Benjamin Jowett*, eds Evelyn Abbot and Lewis Campbell, vol.II (1893)

W6/5749

≪ 13 June ≫

They Liked Ritual

Ordered movement, ritual, is natural to men. But some ages are better at it, are more used to it, and more sensitive to it, than others. The Middle Ages like great spectacle, and therefore (if for no other reasons – but there were many) they liked ritual. They talked in ritual – blazons declared it. They were nourished by ritual – the Eucharist exhibited it. They made love by ritual – the convention of courtly love preserved it. Certainly also they did all these things without ritual – but ritual (outside the inner experience) was the norm. And ritual maintains and increases that natural sense of the significance of movement. And, of course, of formulae, of words.

Charles Williams, *Witchcraft* (1941)

2003.c.21

❧ 14 June ❧

Where Magic is Believed in

Hegel has very correctly pointed out that where magic is believed in, not everyone is able or allowed to practise it. Special individuals are chosen on account of their superior knowledge of the formulae, methods of operation, etc., believed to prevail with the powers which it is sought to persuade. This select body of men corresponds to the priests, which in the lower forms of religion are credited with extraordinary knowledge of Divine secrets, and with unusual influence over Deity. Indeed, it is hard to say when exactly the magician resigns, and the priest enters upon office. To some extent the conception and conduct which properly belong to magic, accompany religion in all its historical forms.

T. Witton Davies, *Magic, Divination, and Demonology Among the Hebrews and Their Neighbours* (1898)

08631.g.16

❧ 15 June ❧

The Duty of Adequate Inquiry

Theoretically, the duty of adequate inquiry into the truth of any statement of serious importance before believing it is universally admitted. Practically, no duty is more universally neglected.

Walter R. Cassels, *Supernatural Religion: An Inquiry into the Reality of Divine Revelation* (1874)

4017.i.21

≪ 16 June ≫

Faults in this Thing

There are an hundred faults in this Thing, and an hundred things might be said to prove them beauties. But it is needless. A book may be amusing with numerous errors, or it may be very dull without a single absurdity. The hero of this piece unites in himself the three greatest characters upon earth; he is a priest, an husbandman, and the father of a family. He is drawn as ready to teach, and ready to obey, as simple in affluence, and majestic in adversity. In this age of opulence and refinement whom can such a character please? Such as are fond of high life, will turn with disdain from the simplicity of his country fire-side. Such as mistake ribaldry for humour, will find no wit in his harmless conversation; and such as have been taught to deride religion, will laugh at one whose chief stores of comfort are drawn from futurity.

Oliver Goldsmith, 'Advertisment', *The Vicar of Wakefield* (1766)

12613.bbb.15

≪ 17 June ≫

Deliberate Falsehoods

By the time I went to this day-school my taste for natural history, and more especially for collecting, was well developed. I tried to make out the names of plants, and collected all sorts of things, shells, seals, franks, coins, and minerals. The passion for collecting which leads a man to be a systematic naturalist, a virtuoso, or a miser, was very strong in me, and was clearly innate, as none of my sisters or brother ever had this taste.

One little event during this year has fixed itself very firmly in my mind, and I hope that it has done so from my conscience having been afterwards sorely troubled by it; it is curious as showing that apparently I was interested at this early age in the variability of plants! I told another little boy (I believe it was Leighton, who afterwards became a well-known lichenologist and botanist), that I could produce variously coloured polyanthuses and primroses by watering them with certain coloured fluids, which was of course a monstrous fable, and had never been tried by me. I may here also confess that as a little boy I was much given to inventing deliberate falsehoods, and this was always done for the sake of causing excitement. For instance, I once gathered much valuable fruit from my father's trees and hid it in the shrubbery, and then ran in breathless haste to spread the news that I had discovered a hoard of stolen fruit.

Charles Darwin, *The Life and Letters of Charles Darwin,*
Including an autobiographical chapter,
vol.I, ed. Francis Darwin (1887)

10859.g.27

❦ 18 June ❧

Yes, I Have Lied

Yes, I have lied, and so must walk my way,
Bearing the liar's curse upon my head;
Letting my weak and sickly heart be fed
On food which does the present craving stay,
But may be clean-denied me e'en today,
And though 'twere certain, yet were ought but bread;
Letting – for so they say, it seems, I said,
And I am all too weak to disobey!
Therefore for me sweet Nature's scenes reveal not
Their charm; sweet Music greets me and I feel not;
Sweet eyes pass off me uninspired; yea, more,
The golden tide of opportunity
Flows wafting-in friendships and better, – I
Unseeing, listless, pace along the shore.

Arthur Hugh Clough,
from a series of poems titled 'Blank Misgivings of a Creature
moving about in Worlds not realised', in Poems (1849)
11644.eeee.45

⫷ 19 June ⫸

The Only Effect

If art does not enlarge men's sympathies, it does nothing morally. [...] the only effect I ardently long to produce by my writings is that those who read them should be better able to imagine and to feel the pains and joys of those who differ from themselves in everything but the broad fact of being struggling, erring, human creatures.

George Eliot, letter, 5 July 1859,
in *George Eliot's life as related in her letters and journals*,
vol.II, ed. J. W. Cross (1886)
10854.e.14

⫷ 20 June ⫸

And Then the Queen Died of Grief

'The king died and then the queen died', is a story.
'The king died and then the queen died of grief' is a plot.

E. M. Forster,
Aspects of the Novel (1927)
823 *4203*

⤶ 21 June *⤷*

The Bosom of the Darkest Woods

To make anything very terrible, obscurity seems in general to be necessary. When we know the full extent of any danger, when we can accustom our eyes to it, a great deal of the apprehension vanishes. Everyone will be sensible of this who considers how greatly night adds to our dread in all cases of danger, and how much the notions of ghosts and goblins (of which none can form clear ideas) affect minds, which give credit to the popular tales concerning such sorts of beings.

Those despotic governments which are founded on the passions of men – and principally upon the passion of fear – keep their chief as much as may be from the public eye. The policy has been the same in many cases of religion; almost all the heathen temples were dark. Even in the barbarous temples of the Americans at this day, they keep their idol in a dark part of the hut, which is consecrated to his worship. For this purpose too the druids performed all their ceremonies in the bosom of the darkest woods, and in the shade of the oldest and most spreading oaks.

Edmund Burke, *A Philosophical Enquiry into the Origins of our Ideas of the Sublime and Beautiful* (1757)

11805.ccc.17

❮ 22 June ❯

A Misty Profundity

It is a safe rule to apply that, when a mathematical or philosophical author writes with a misty profundity, he is talking nonsense.

A. N. Whitehead, *An Introduction to Mathematics* (1911)

510 *2048*

❮ 23 June ❯

Death-Drunkenness

June 12, 1916

The Dadaist fights against the death-throes and death-drunkenness of his time. Averse to every clever reticence, he cultivates the curiosity of one who experiences delight even in the most questionable forms of insubordination. He knows that this world of systems has gone to pieces, and that the age which demanded cash has organised a bargain sale of godless philosophies.

Hugo Ball, from *Die Flucht aus der Zeit* (1927), trans. Eugene Jonas, in *transition* 25 (Fall 1936)

Cup.400.a.30

☙ 24 June ❧

Consider Your Own Situation

LONDON, May 27, O. S. 1748

DEAR BOY: This and the two next years make so important a period of your life, that I cannot help repeating to you my exhortations, my commands, and (what I hope will be still more prevailing with you than either) my earnest entreaties, to employ them well. Every moment that you now lose, is so much character and advantage lost; as, on the other hand, every moment that you now employ usefully, is so much time wisely laid out, at most prodigious interest. These two years must lay the foundations of all the knowledge that you will ever have; you may build upon them afterward as much as you please, but it will be too late to lay any new ones. Let me beg of you, therefore, to grudge no labor nor pains to acquire, in time, that stock of knowledge, without which you never can rise, but must make a very insignificant figure in the world. Consider your own situation; you have not the advantage of rank or fortune to bear you up; I shall, very probably, be out of the world before you can properly be said to be in it. What then will you have to rely on but your own merit? That alone must raise you, and that alone will raise you, if you have but enough of it. I have often heard and read of oppressed and unrewarded merit, but I have oftener (I might say always) seen great merit make its way, and meet with its reward, to a certain degree at least, in spite of all difficulties. By merit, I mean the moral virtues, knowledge, and manners; as to the moral virtues, I say nothing to you; they speak best for themselves, nor can I suspect that they want any recommendation with you; I will therefore only assure you, that without them you will be most unhappy.

Earl Chesterfield, Letter CLII, *Letters Written by Philip Dormer Earl of Chesterfield To His Son 1737–1768* (1774; 1890 edn)

1509/792

❮ 25 June ❯

Accumulated Knowledge

Remember that accumulated knowledge, like accumulated capital, increases at compound interest: but it differs from the accumulation of capital in this; that the increase of knowledge produces a more rapid rate of progress, whilst the accumulation of capital leads to a lower rate of interest. Capital thus checks its own accumulation: knowledge thus accelerates its own advance. Each generation, therefore, to deserve comparison with its predecessor, is bound to add much more largely to the common stock than that which it immediately succeeds.

Charles Babbage, *The Exposition of 1851;*
or, Views of the Industry, the Science,
and the Government of England (1851)

T 10274

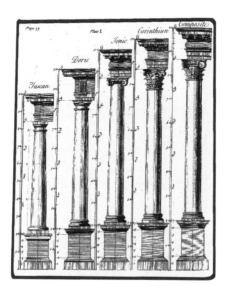

⤺ 26 June ⤻

Scarcely on Speaking Terms

But, once in a way, it is as well to renounce the purely objective life of every day in favour of this other one. Ordinarily, you are scarcely on speaking terms with your real self; you catch hurried glimpses of it, darting before you, out of reach of touch and realization, in the groves and alleys of commonplace concerns, among the brush and underwood of crowding 'things to do,' and you are barely acquaintances. But live alone for awhile, with no special pressing occupation, and how different it is. You have time to think over things that puzzled you, time to look into the conclusions you have had to jump at, leisure to unravel all the tangles that have pained you, opportunity to disinter the reason of your feelings for this and that. It is very good for man or woman to live alone, calmly and quietly, for a period, of whiles; to let their restlessness, their dissatisfaction, and their cares drop from them 'like the needles shaken from out the gusty pine.'

Ménie Muriel Dowie, *A Girl in the Karpathians* (1891)
10215.de.8

≪ 27 June ≫

O Human Face!

A greeting to thee, O most trusty friend!
That has so steadfastly companioned me.
What other, say, in this can equal thee,
Who cam'st to life with me, with me shalt end?
Poor face of mine! Right often dost thou lend
A smile to hide some smile less thoughts that be
Bound deep in heart, and oft thy kind eyes see
My soul's great grief and bid their ears attend.

Ah, childish fairness, seeming near, yet far,
Prized tenderly by dear ones pass'd away,
Fain I'd recall it! Next, an oval grace
Of girlhood; for thy woman's sorrows are
Stamped now on lips and forehead day by day,
Yet God's own image thou – O human face!

Lady (Caroline Blanche Elizabeth) Lindsay,
'To My Own Face', in *Lyrics and Other Poems* (1890)
011653.i.26

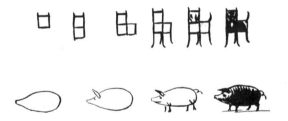

≪ 28 June ≫

Successive Slight Modifications

If it could be demonstrated that any complex organ existed which could not possibly have been formed by successive slight modifications, my theory would absolutely break down.

Charles Darwin, On the Origin of Species
by means of Natural Selection, or the preservation of
favoured races in the struggle for life (1859)
C.113.c.8

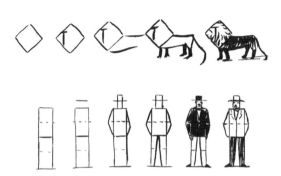

≪ 29 June ≫

Organs and Extensions of the Body

Any invention or technology is an extension or self-amputation of our physical bodies, and such extension also demands new ratios or new equilibriums among the other organs and extensions of the body.

Marshall McLuhan, *Understanding Media:*
The Extensions of Man (1964)
X.529/948

≪ 30 June ≫

Mental Software

The prostheses of the industrial era were still external, *exotecnical*, whereas those we know now are ramified and internalized – *esotechnical*. Ours is the age of soft technologies, the age of genetic and mental software.

Jean Baudrillard, *The Transparency of Evil: Essays on Extreme*
Phenomena [1990], trans. James Benedict (1993)
YK.1994.a.448

JULY

❋ 1 July ❋

The Soil of England

Let us imagine that a portion of the soil of England has been levelled off perfectly and that on it a cartographer traces a map of England. The job is perfect; there is no detail of the soil of England, no matter how minute, that is not registered on the map; everything has there its correspondence. This map, in such a case, should contain a map of the map, which should contain a map of the map, and so on to infinity.

Josiah Royce,
The World and the Individual (1900)

08464.ee.67

❋ 2 July ❋

Perish Such Rules

Another most desirable benefit belonging to a fertile soil is, that states so endowed are not obliged to pay so much attention to that most distressing and disheartening of all cries to every man of humanity – the cry of the master manufacturers and merchants for low wages, to enable them to find a market for their exports. If a country can only be rich by running a successful race for low wages, I should be disposed to say at once, perish such riches.

Thomas Robert Malthus,
*Principles of Political Economy Considered with a
View to their Practical Application* (1820)

1027.e.11

❋ 3 July ❋

Better Than Nothing

If the Treasury were to fill old bottles with banknotes, bury them at suitable depths in disused coalminers which are then filled up to the surface with town rubbish, and leave it to private enterprise on well-tried principles of laissez-faire to dig the notes up again (the right to do so being obtained, of course, by tendering for leases of the note-bearing territory), there need be no more unemployment and, with the help of the repercussions, the real income of the community, and its capital wealth also, would probably become a good deal greater than it actually is. It would, indeed, be more sensible to build houses and the like; but if there are political and practical difficulties in the way of this, the above would be better than nothing.

John Maynard Keynes,
The General Theory of Employment Interest and Money (1936)
Cup.403.h.31

❋ 4 July ❋

Each Red Brick

I remember a back-drop of a brick wall I painted for a play. I painted each red brick by hand. Afterwards it occurred to me that I could just have painted the whole thing red and put in the white lines.

Joe Brainard, *I Remember* [1970–] (complete new edn, 2001)
YA.2001.a.40359

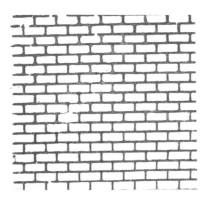

✹ 5 July ✹

Human Want and Misery

Ah, so much is said about human want and misery – I seek to understand it, I have also some acquaintance with it at close range; so much is said about wasted lives – but only that man's life is wasted who lived on, so deceived by the joys of life or by its sorrows that he never became eternally and decisively conscious of himself as spirit, as self, or (what is the same thing) never became aware and in the deepest sense received an impression of the fact that there is a God, and that he, he himself, his self, exists before this God, this gain of infinity, which is never attained except through despair.

Soren Kierkegaard, *The Sickness unto Death* (1849),
trans. Walter Lowrie (1941)
W 49/214

✹ 6 July ✹

When I Shall Be Dead

When I shall be dead, the principles, of which I am composed, will still perform their part in the universe, and will be equally useful in the grand fabric, as when they composed this individual creature. The difference to the whole will be no greater than betwixt my being in a chamber and in the open air. The one change is of more importance to me than the other; but no more so to the universe.

David Hume, 'Of Suicide', in *Essays on suicide, and the immortality of the soul, ascribed to the late David Hume, Esq. Never before published. With remarks, intended as an antidote to the poison contained in these performances, by the editor* (1755; 1783)
1509/3492

✵ 7 July ✵

Do People Moulder Equally

Do People moulder equally,
They bury, in the Grave?

Emily Dickinson, manuscript *c.*1862, in
The Poems of Emily Dickinson, ed. R. W. Franklin, vol.I (1999)

YK.1999.b.8190

✵ 8 July ✵

A Show of Hands

The question whether our conscious personality survives
after death has been answered by almost all races of men
in the affirmative. On this point sceptical or agnostic
people are nearly, if not wholly, unknown. Accordingly, if
abstract truth could be determined, like the gravest issues
of national policy, by a show of hands or a counting of
heads, the doctrine of human immortality, or at least of
a life after death, would deserve to rank among the most
firmly established of truths; for were the question put to
the vote of the whole mankind there can be no doubt that
the 'ayes' would have it by an overwhelming majority. The
few dissenters would be overborne; their voices would be
drowned in the general roar.

James Frazer, *The Belief in Immortality
and the Worship of the Dead*, vol.I (1913)

T 12941

✻ 9 July ✻

When I Shall Be Dead

My son's Christian name was Vincent. This is only the second time I have dared to write it. He died at the close of October, in the year 1852, and was buried in beautiful Kensal Green, my own final bed-chamber, I trust, in this world, towards which I often look in my solitary walks, with eyes at once most melancholy, yet consoled. [...] It was a colder break of dawn than usual, but equally beautiful, as if, in both respects, it came to take him away, when my son died. His last words were poetry itself. A glass of water had been given him at his request; and on feeling of it, he said, 'I drink the morning.'

And there are those who would persuade us that this beautiful soul will never be seen by us more! Could space then be filled? so that there should nowhere be any room for the sould? That is impossible. And must not beauty exist, as long as there are stars, and their orderly movements anywhere? That is certain. Why then should any such portions of beauty perish, when there is no need of their perishing? And why should they not live on, and drink up those tears as they did the morning, since God has so made us long for it, when he need not have done so? As the tendency to sleep is the augury and harbinger of sleep, so desire like this – let us be sure of it – is the augury and harbinger of what it has been made to desire. Do we suppose that God makes manifest halves of anything, without intending the remainders?

Leigh Hunt,
The Autobiography of Leigh Hunt (1860)
2408.aa.2

✹ 10 July ✹

We Disagree Invincibly and Finally

To sum up, then, the immortality which I hold to be desirable, and which I suggest to you as desirable, is one in which a continuity of experience analogous to that which we are aware of here is carried on into a life after death, the essence of that life being the continuous unfolding, no doubt through stress and conflict, of those potentialities of Good of which we aware here as the most significant part of ourselves. I hold that the desirability of this is a matter of plain fact, and that in putting it forward I am giving no evidence of superstition, weakness, or egotism, but on the contrary am recognizing the deepest element in human nature. Some of you, probably, will agree with this; others will strongly disagree; and to those who disagree I have no further arguments to address; we disagree invincibly and finally.

G. Lowes Dickinson, *Religion and Immortality* (1911)

4257.e.45

✹ 11 July ✹

Something We Do Continuously

Dying is something we human beings do continuously, not just at the end of our physical lives on this earth.

Dr Elisabeth Kübler-Ross,
Death: The Final Stage of Growth (1975)

79/23873

✹ 12 July ✹

I Don't Think Much of It

If this is dying, then I don't think much of it.

Lytton Strachey, q. in Michael Holroyd,
Lytton Strachey: A Biography (1968)
X.900/7490

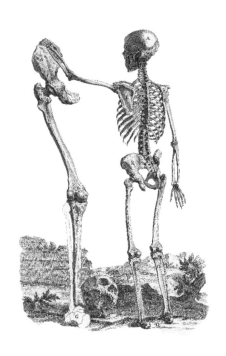

13 July

From Bedde to Flore

How Death comes
Wanne mine eyhnen misten,
And mine heren sissen,
And my nose coldet,
And my tunge foldet,
And my rude slaket,
And mine lippes blaken,
And my muth grennet,
And my spotel rennet,
And mine her riset,
And mine herte griset,
And mine honden bivien,
And mine fet stivien –
Al to late! Al to late!
Wanne the bere is ate gate.

Thanne I schel flutte
From bedde to flore,
From flore to here,
From here to bere,
From bere to putte,
And te putt fordut.
Thanne lyd mine hus uppe mine nose.
Of all this world ne give I it a pese!

Anonymous thirteenth century lyric,
in *Medieval English Lyrics*, ed. R. T. Davies (1963)
11663.p.36

❋ 14 July ❋

The Whites of Eggs

If I had my life over again I should form the habit of nightly composing myself to thoughts of death. I would practise, as it were, the remembrance of death. There is no other practice which so intensifies life. Death, when it approaches, ought not to take one by surprise. It should be part of the full expectancy of life. Without an ever-present sense of death life is insipid. You might as well live on the whites of eggs.

Muriel Spark, *Memento Mori* (1959)
NNN.13216

❋ 15 July ❋

An Indefinite Froth

Sometimes in dreams the dream becomes palpably more substantial. The process is like scrambling eggs. From an indefinite froth comes, seemingly instantaneously, something with a recognizable texture, something one can put in one's mouth. When a dream behaves in this way, it is becoming a work of art. The effect is often one of healthy bathos. From a sickly-sweet twilight of indefinite sensations there emerges perhaps the exceedingly familiar, exceedingly detailed, figure of someone one knows, and this at once makes the dialectic of the dream concrete.

Louis MacNeice, 'Sir Thomas Malory', in
The English Novelists: A Survey of the Novel by Twenty
Contemporary Novelists, ed. Derek Verschoyle (1936)
W.49/2742

❋ 16 July ❋

The Pigmentation of Fact

Dreams have only the pigmentation of fact.

Djuna Barnes, *Nightwood* (1936)

❋ 17 July ❋

The Imagination of Dreamers

It is a common error of the people who are called wise and practical in ordinary times, to judge by certain rules the men whose very object is to change or to destroy those rules. When a time is come at which passion takes the guidance of affairs, the beliefs of men of experience are less worthy of consideration than the schemes which engage the imagination of dreamers.

Alexis De Tocqueville, *On the State of Society in France Before the Revolution of 1789*, trans. H. Reeve (1873)

944.03 *4891*

❋ 18 July ❋

The Gate of Polished Horn

[…] dreams verily are baffling and unclear of meaning, and in no wise do they find fulfilment in all things for men. For two are the gates of shadowy dreams, and one is fashioned of horn and one of ivory. Those dreams that pass through the gate of sawn ivory deceive men, bringing words that find no fulfilment. But those that come forth through the gate of polished horn bring true issues to pass, when any mortal sees them.

Homer, *The Odyssey*,
c. eighth century BCE, trans. A.T. Murray (1919)

2282.d.53

✸ 19 July ✸

Not Even the Smallest Measure of Success

To the enormous majority of persons who risk themselves in literature, not even the smallest measure of success can fall. They had better take to some other profession as quickly as may be, they are only making a sure thing of disappointment, only crowding the narrow gates of fortune and fame. [...] If literature and occupation with letters were not its own reward, truly they who seem to succeed might envy those who fail. It is not wealth that they win, as fortunate men in other professions count wealth; it is not rank nor fashion that come to their call nor come to call on them. Their success is to be let dwell with their own fancies, or with the imaginations of others far greater than themselves; their success is this living in fantasy; a little remote from the hubbub and the contests of the world. At the best they will be vexed by curious eyes and idle tongues, at the best they will die not rich in this world's goods, yet not unconsoled by the friendships which they win among me and women whose faces they will never see. They may well be content, and thrice content, with their lot, yet it is not a lot which should provoke envy, nor be coveted by ambition.

It is not an easy goal to attain, as the crowd of aspirants dream, nor is the reward luxurious when it is attained. A garland, usually fading and not immortal, has to be run for, not without dust and heat.

Andrew Lang,
How to Fail in Literature: A Lecture (1890)

11850.aaaa.36

✿ 20 July ✿

The Master of an Ordinary

An author ought to consider himself, not as a gentleman who gives a private or eleemosynary treat, but rather as one who keeps a public ordinary, at which all persons are welcome for their money. In the former case, it is well known that the entertainer provides what fare he pleases; and though this should be very indifferent, and utterly disagreeable to the taste of his company, they must not find any fault; nay, on the contrary, good breeding forces them outwardly to approve and to commend whatever is set before them. Now the contrary of this happens to the master of an ordinary. Men who pay for what they eat will insist on gratifying their palates, however nice and whimsical these may prove; and if everything is not agreeable to their taste, will challenge a right to censure, to abuse, and to d—n their dinner without controul. [...] The provision, then, which we have here made is no other than Human Nature. Nor do I fear that my sensible reader, though most luxurious in his taste, will start, cavil, or be offended, because I have named but one article. The tortoise – as the alderman of Bristol, well learned in eating, knows by much experience – besides the delicious calipash and calipee, contains many different kinds of food; nor can the learned reader be ignorant, that in human nature, though here collected under one general name, is such prodigious variety, that a cook will have sooner gone through all the several species of animal and vegetable food in the world, than an author will be able to exhaust so extensive a subject.

Henry Fielding,
from 'The Introduction to the work, or bill of fare to the feast',
in *The History of Tom Jones, a Foundling* (1749)

1472.aa.28

❋ 21 July ❋

A Hundred Voices Screaming Out

All was mute, except a hundred voices screaming out, Brickdust! – Knives to grind! – Scissors to grind! – Come buy my water-cresses! – New laid eggs, five a groat! Crack 'em and try 'em, five a groat! – Work for the cooper! – Come buy my pret-pret-pretty level jem-em-ememmy sticks, or sticks to dust your cloaths! – Mu-u-uke! – Maids below! – Hot mutton pies, hot! – Maids below! – Hot mutton pies, hot! – Buy my cod, dainty live cod! [...] Fine China oranges! – Curds and whey! – buy my curds and whey! – Flummery! buy my flummery! – Buy my roasted pig! a long-tailed pig, or a short-tailed pig, or a pig without even a tail! – Hot nice dumplings hot! Diddle, diddle, diddle, diddle ... dumplings ho-o-t!

London street cries, in
Miss C-Y's Cabinet of Curiosities; Or, The Green Room broke open.
By Tristram Shandy, Gent. (1765)
641.e.24.(6.)

❋ 22 July ❋

Strange Literary Pastures

A mind endowed with an insatiable curiosity as to all things knowable and unknowable; an imagination which tinges with poetical hues the vast accumulation of incoherent facts thus stored in a capacious memory; and a strangely vivid humour that is always detecting the quaintest analogies, and, as it were, striking light from the most unexpected collocations of uncompromising materials: such talents are by themselves enough to provide a man with work for life, and to make all his work delightful. To them, moreover, we must add a disposition absolutely incapable of controversial bitterness; 'a constitution,' as he says of himself, 'so general that it consorts and sympathises with all things;' an absence of all antipathies to loathsome objects in nature – to French 'dishes of snails, frogs, and toadstools,' or to Jewish repasts on 'locusts or grasshoppers;' an equal toleration – which in the first half of the seventeenth century is something astonishing – for all theological systems; an admiration even of our natural enemies, the French, the Spaniards, the Italians, and the Dutch; a love of all climates, of all countries; and, in short, an utter incapacity to 'absolutely detest or hate any essence except the devil.' [...] The best mode of approaching so original a writer is to examine the intellectual food on which his mind was nourished. He dwelt by preference in strange literary pastures; and their nature will let us into some secrets as to his taste and character.

Leslie Stephen, 'Sir Thomas Browne',
in *Hours in a Library* (1876)
W27/9932

✾ 23 July ✾

Some More of this Trifle?

The great evil of the advanced state of society in which we live, is that moderate enjoyments are too little valued, and things only of the highest relish will please our pampered and vitiated appetites. Amusement has changed into dissipation, Convenience into Luxury, Elegance to Splendour; Ideas of opulence have passed all bounds of modest computation, and the wealth of a province is scarcely enough for a London Counting-house [...] Such prodigious preparation [...] instead of being a compliment to our guests, is really nothing better than a direct offence; – is it not a tacit insinuation that YOU think it absolutely necessary to bribe the depravity of their palates, when you desire the pleasure of their Company? [...] Instead of, 'Do let me send you some more of this Mock Turtle' – 'Another Patty' – 'Sir, some more of this Trifle,' 'I MUST INSIST upon your trying this nice Melon;' the language of hospitality should rather run thus: – 'Shall I send you a fit of the Cholic, Sir?' 'Pray let me have the pleasure of giving you a Pain in your Stomach.' 'Sir, let me help you to a little gentle bilious head-Ache.' 'Ma'am, you surely cannot refuse a touch of Inflammation of the Bowels.'

William Kitchiner, *The Housekeeper's Oracle; or, art of domestic management: containing a complete system of carving with accuracy and elegance; hints relative to dinner parties; the art of managing servants and the economist and epicure's calendar; shewing the seasons where all kinds of meat, fish, poultry, game, vegetables and fruits, first arrive in the market – earliest time forces – when most plentiful – and when best and cheapest* (1829).

1136.l.25

✳ 24 July ✳

Oysters and Champagne in My Mother's Womb

The character of a child is already plain even in its mother's womb. Before I was born, my mother was in great agony of spirit and in a tragic situation. She could take no food except iced oysters and iced champagne. If people ask me when I began to dance, I reply, 'In my mother's womb, probably as a result of the oysters and champagne – the food of Aphrodite.'

Isadora Duncan, *My Life* (1927)

YH.1986.a.76

✳ 25 July ✳

Pain After Food

The natural process of gastric digestion consists in mechanical and chemical alterations in the food introduced into the stomach, by which it is fitted for absorption, or for discharge through the pyloric orifice into the duodenum; and it is accompanied by certain movements of the stomach itself, and of the intestines, and by the secretion into the cavity and admixture with the food of fluids necessary to effect the alterations referred to. It is unaccompanied by pain or uneasiness.

Edward Ballard, *On Pain After Food: its causes and treatment* (1854)

7440.b.1

✳ 26 July ✳

So-called 'Ladies Who Lunch'

About twice a year I make a plan to meet one friend or another for lunch. We choose a pub or café with good food but we eat little or maybe don't actually eat at all. Strictly what we are doing is meeting at lunch but not for it. I read somewhere that even so-called 'ladies who lunch' do not lunch in the ingesting sense of the word. They go to fashionable restaurants and sip sparkly water. They order leaves done up extravagantly with balsamic vinegar and see-through shavings of Parmesan and when they arrive note how pretty they are. Then with a fork they prod them a bit this way and that, delicately drooling, but the prodding is really for the sport of rearrangement, as if the ingredients were a set of lacy cushions on a day bed needing to be scattered just so. I don't go out to lunch because I have tamed my appetite not to be unleashed till later in the day. I do not eat it because I am generally on my own at that time so there are no questions asked. Lunch is a great deal easier to dodge than dinner.

Candida Crewe, *Eating Myself* (2006)
YK.2006.a.14682

※ 27 July ※

Our Domestic Happiness

Good apple pies are a considerable part of our domestic happiness.

Jane Austen, letter to Cassandra Austen, 17/18 October 1815,
in *Jane Austen's Letters*, ed. Deirdre Le Faye (1995)
YC.1995.a.1430

※ 28 July ※

Human Deglutition

Feeling without judgement is a washy draught indeed; but judgement untempered by feeling is too bitter and husky a morsel for human deglutition.

Currer Bell [Charlotte Brontë],
Jane Eyre: An Autobiography (1847)
C.70.d.13

❋ 29 July ❋

Some Liquid They Used to Drink

DAVID GREENBERGER: Is coffee mentioned in the Bible?

LARRY GREEN: No, I don't think so. Milk, milk and honey, that's the lord's supper. Before they killed him they gave him a big meal. They said to him, 'That's the last meal you'll get for the rest of your life.'

ABE SURGECOFF: They had some, ah, some, some liquid, some liquid they used to drink, but I don't know what the liquid was.

ERNIE BROOKINGS: To my knowledge, no.

FRANK KANSLASKY: I don't read it, how do I know?

BILL NIEMI: It might be, but I'm not sure. It probably is mentioned once. Some of them that write them bibles leave more to the imagination so you can make sermons out of it. It would probably be in Lazarus. Lazarus had two sisters, Martha and Mary.

VILJO LEHTO: Yeah, it is at one time. It's dope. If you're drinkin' coffee you're not religious, you're a dope! It comes off a tree from a bean you know.

DG: You drink coffee.

VILJO: Sometimes I do, not always. I drink instant coffee, decaffeinated. If you drink coffee it affects your heart you know, it's not good for your heart.

WALLY BAKER: Not that I know of. A lot of wine mentioned.

JOHN HODOROWSKI: Sure. At least, that's what I was told, but you hear a lot of bullshit.

GEORGE VROOMAN: No, wine and strong drink is all I know of. I don't know what the strong drink was.

David Greenberger, *Tell Me If I've Stopped: Voices from the Duplex Planet* (1993)

YK.1996.a.6659

THE COFFEE STALL

❋ 3o July ❋

A Strong Solution of Books

Society is a strong solution of books. It draws its virtue out of what is best worth reading, as hot water draws the strength of tea-leaves. If I were a prince, I would hire or buy a private literary tea-pot, in which I would steep all the leaves of new books that promised well. The infusion would do for me without the vegetable fibre.

Oliver Wendell Holmes,
The Autocrat of the Breakfast-Table (1858)
1233.e.12

❊ 31 July ❊

A Library Cormorant

I am, & ever have been, a great reader – & have read almost everything – a library cormorant – I am *deep* in all out-of-the-way books, whether of the monkish times or of the puritanical aera – I have read & digested most of the Historical Writers; but I do not *like* history. Metaphysics & Poetry and 'Facts of Mind' (i.e. Accounts of all strange phantasms that ever possessed your philosophy-dreamers; from Thoth, the Egyptian to Taylor the English pagan) are my darling Studies. – In short, I seldom read except to amuse myself – & I am almost always reading – Of useful knowledge, I am a so-so chemist, & I love chemistry – all else is *blank* – but I *will* be (please God) an Horticulturalist and a Farmer.

Samuel Taylor Coleridge, letter to John Thelwall, 19 November 1796, q. in *The Road to Xanadu: A Study in the Strange Ways of Imagination*, John Livingston-Lowes (1927)

011824.c.1

AUGUST

⚓ 1 August ⚓

Straängen Fond o' the Jam

'Why, Mr. Alfred; you know Mr. Alfred. Ivvery one, in those daäys, knew Mr. Alfred hereabout howivver. You've heard tell of Mr Alfred Tennyson, the owd doctor's son [...] He was straängen fond o' the jam as well as the peärs, was Mr. Alfred. My missus ud saäy, "Now here's Mr. Alfred a 'coomin; we must git the jam ready" [...] We haven't heard of him for years, but he grew up a straängen greät man, I suppose and addles his bread by his writings; is worth some hundreds, they do saäy.'

'Yes,' I said, 'I should think you might almost say he is worth some thousands, and not hundreds. He is the greatest poet of the land, and the Queen wishes to make him a grand lord for his work as a poet.'

I shall not soon forget the astonishment that came into the old man's face, as, hobbling to the back-kitchen door, he said, 'Missus, do you hear what this young gentleman is saäying about Mr. Alfred? He saäys he's wuth thousands by his potry!'

'Naäy, naäy, sir, you mun be mistäen; sewerly it's hundreds, not thousands. Well I nivver! Why you know i' them daäys, we thowt he wur daft. He was allus ramblin' off quite by hissen wi'out a coat to his back and wi'out a hat to his head, nor nowt [...] i'them daäys we all thowt he was craäzed. Well, well! An the Queen wants to maäke him a lord, poor thing! Well, I nivver did hear the likes of that for sarten sewerness'.

Canon Hardwicke Drummond Rawnsley,
Memories of the Tennysons (1900)

10827.e.17

2 August

Keeping Everything, For Better or Worse

Thomas Edison once said that genius was one per cent inspiration and ninety-nine per cent perspiration. Genius apart, my quota of inspiration came one Sunday twenty-five years ago, on 8 September 1963. I was in Inverness, mid-journey from Edinburgh to the very north of Scotland, when the pangs of hunger prompted me to find something to eat. My search ended with the purchase of a pack of Mackintosh's Munchies and a pack of McVitie's Ginger Nut biscuits, both from a vending machine as there were no shops open on a Sunday afternoon. It suddenly dawned on me, while consuming the Munchies, that when I threw the Munchies pack away, I would also be throwing away a small fragment of history.

Furthermore, the thought occurred to me that if I was to save the wrappers, tins and bottles from every product I bought, collectively they would represent a social history of life in Britain. I knew from my childhood experience of collecting Lesney 'Matchbox' miniature die-cast toys and from my research into philatelic postal stationery, that there was continual change. Pack designs would be updated, new products would arrive, others disappear, and the advertisements for the products would tell of other aspects of social change. From that moment on I was to keep everything – for better or for worse.

Robert Opie, *Sweet Memories:*
A Selection of Confectionery Delights (1988; repr. 1999)

YK.1999.a.7980

⚒ 3 August ⚒

Nonseriously

When we can begin to take our failures nonseriously, it means we are ceasing to be afraid of them. It is of immense importance to learn to laugh at ourselves.

Katherine Mansfield, *Journal of Katherine Mansfield*, ed. J. Middleton Murray (1927)

W52/7635

⚜ 4 August ⚜

Pour in the Flummery

To make Flummery

Put one ounce of bitter and one of sweet almonds into a basin, pour over them some boiling water to make the skins come off, which is called blanching. Strip off the skins and throw the kernels into cold water. Then take them out and beat them in a marble mortar with a little rosewater to keep them from oiling. When they are beat, put them into a pint of calf's foot stock, set it over the fire and sweeten it to your taste with loaf sugar. As soon as it boils strain it through a piece of muslin or gauze. When a little cold put it into a pint of thick cream and keep stirring it often till it grows thick and cold. Wet your moulds in cold water and pour in the flummery, let it stand five or six hours at least before you turn them out. If you make the flummery stiff and wet the moulds, it will turn out without putting it into warm water, for water takes off the figures of the mould and makes the flummery look dull.

N.B. Be careful you keep stirring it till cold or it will run in lumps when you turn it out of the mould.

Elizabeth Raffald, *The Experienced English Housekeeper, For the Use and Ease of Ladies, Housekeepers, Cooks, &c* (1769)

1037.g.23

Boiled Puddings.

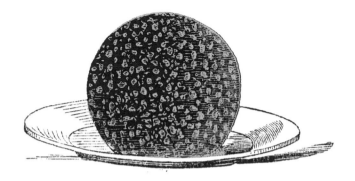

GENERAL DIRECTIONS.

⚜ 5 August ⚜

Lawyers in Charge

The role of lawyers in selecting research projects and methodologies and controlling the dissemination of results is, perhaps, the most important insight offered by the documents. The industry's increasing reliance on lawyers to manage research reveals an industry policy toward research that was adversarial and elevated advocacy over objectivity. By putting lawyers in charge of scientific research, the tobacco companies effectively adopted a research policy that had nothing to do with finding out and disseminating the truth about the health effects of tobacco or with sponsoring truly independent research on that subject. It had everything to do with protecting the political and legal position of the industry and protecting its profits.

Stanton. A. Glantz, John Slade, Lisa A. Bero, Peter Hanauer, Deborah E. Barnes, *The Cigarette Papers* (1996)

YC.1996.b.4625

⚜ 6 August ⚜

The Great Advantages of Simulation and Dissimulation

The great advantages of simulation and dissimulation are three. First, to lay asleep opposition, and to surprise. For where a man's intentions are published, it is an alarum to call up all that are against them. The second is, to reserve to a man's self a fair retreat. For if a man engage himself by a manifest declaration, he must go through or take a fall. The third is, the better to discover the mind of another. For to him that opens himself men will hardly show themselves adverse; but will fair let him go on, and turn their freedom of speech to freedom of thought. And therefore it is a good shrewd proverb of the Spaniard, Tell a lie and find a troth. As if there were no way of discovery but by simulation. There be also three disadvantages, to set it even. The first, that simulation and dissimulation commonly carry with them a show of fearfulness, which in any business doth spoil the feathers of round flying up to the mark. The second is that it puzzleth and perplexth the conceits of many, that perhaps would otherwise co-operate with him; and makes a man walk almost alone to his own ends. The third and greatest is, that it depriveth a man of one of the most principal instruments for action; which is trust and belief. The best composition and temperature is to have openness in fame and opinion; secrecy in habit; dissimulation in seasonable use; and a power to feign, if there be no remedy.

Francis Bacon, 'Of Simulation and Dissimulation' (1625), repr. in *The Works of Francis Bacon*, vol.2, eds Robert Leslie Ellis, W. H. D. Rouse, James Spedding (1905)

12204.p.2/28

≈ 7 August ≈

Unaccountable

Freedom means *chance*; you are free, because there is no reason which will account for your particular acts, because no one in the world, not even yourself, can possibly say what you will, or will not, do next. You are 'accountable', in short, because you are a wholly 'unaccountable' creature.

We can not escape this conclusion. If we always can do anything, or nothing, under any circumstances, or merely if, of given alternatives, we can always choose either, then it is always possible that any act should come from any man.

F. H. Bradley, *Ethical Studies* (1876)

8409.c.3

8 August

The Only Freedom I Care About

I protest that if some great Power would agree to make me always think what is true and do what is right, on condition of being turned into a sort of clock and wound up every morning before I got out of bed, I should instantly close with the offer. The only freedom I care about is the freedom to do right; the freedom to do wrong I am ready to part with on the cheapest terms to any one who will take it of me.

Thomas H. Huxley, *Lay Sermons,*
Addresses and Reviews (1870)

12273.h.3

9 August

What Roman Catholics Believe

'Are you really a Roman Catholic?' I asked my aunt with interest. She replied promptly and seriously, 'Yes, my dear, only I just don't believe in all the things they believe in.'

Graham Greene,
Travels with My Aunt (1969)

Nov.14787

⚹ 10 August ⚹

A Queer-bird

An Abram-man.

An abram-man is he that walketh bare-armed, and bare-legged, and feigneth himself mad, and carryeth a pack of wool, or a stick with bacon on it, or suchlike toy, and nameth himself Poor Tom.

A Ruffler.

A ruffler goeth with a weapon to seek service, saying he hath been a servitor in the wars, and beggeth for his relief. But his chiefest trade is to rob poor wayfaring men and market women.

A Prigman.

A prigman goeth with a stick in his hand like an idle person. His property is to steal clothes of the hedge, which they call storing of the rogueman; or else filch poultry, carrying them to the ale-house, which they call the bousing inn, and there sit playing at cards and dice, till that is spent which they have so filched.

[...]

A Queer-bird.

A queer-bird is one that came lately out of prison and goeth to seek service. He is commonly a stealer of horses, which they term a prigger of palfreys.

John Awdeley, from *The Fraternity of Vagabonds. As well of ruffling vagabonds as of beggarly, of women, as of men, of girls as of boys, with their proper names and qualities. With a description of the crafty company of Cozeners and Shifters. [Whereunto also is adjoined the Twenty-five Orders of Knaves, otherwise called a Quartern of Knaves. Confirmed for ever by Cock Lorel.].* repr. in *The Elizabethan Underworld: A collection of Tudor and early Stuart tracts and ballads telling of the lives and misdoings of vagabonds, thieves, rogues and cozeners, and giving some account of the operation of the criminal law,* A. V. Judges (1930)

9502.d.18

11 August

The Life in the Town

The life in the town is a test of man's ability to adjust himself. It tells the story of his skill in living with others, his ability to go out to others and to let others be a part of his own life. You have to go on living with your neighbors. If they are sometimes queer it may be that they also think of you as queer. Without knowing it, you may yourself be one of the 'characters' of your town.

Sherwood Anderson, *Home Town* (1940)

10107.i.41

12 August

The Insatiable Desire for Play

The classical city promoted play with careful solicitude, building the theater and stadium as it built the market place and the temple. The Greeks held their games so integral a part of religion and patriotism that they came to expect from their poets the highest utterances at the very moments when the sense of pleasure released the national life. In the medieval city the knights held their tourneys, the guilds their pageants, the people their dances, and the church made festival for its most cherished saints with gay street processions, and presented a drama in which no less a theme than the history of creation became a matter of thrilling interest. Only in the modern city have men concluded that it is no longer necessary for the municipality to provide for the insatiable desire for play.

Jane Addams, *The Spirit of Youth and the City Streets* (1909)

08415.de.23

Feminist Landscape Architecture

I think one of the primary goals of a feminist landscape architecture would be to work toward a public landscape in which we can roam the streets at midnight, in which every square is available for Virginia Woolf to make up her novels.

Rebecca Solnit,
Storming the Gates of Paradise (2007)

m07/.23042

14 August

Blocks Out of a Box

The schools were newly built, and there were so many of them all over the country, that one might have thought the whole were but one restless edifice with the locomotive gift of Aladdin's palace. They were in a neighbourhood which looked like a toy neighbourhood taken in blocks out of a box by a child of particularly incoherent mind, and set up anyhow; here, one side of a new street; there, a large solitary public-house facing nowhere; here, another finished street already in ruins; there, a church; here, an immense new warehouse; there, a dilapidated old country villa; then a medley of black ditch, sparkling cucumber-frame, rank field, richly cultivated kitchen garden, brick viaduct, arch-spanned canal, and disorder of frowziness and fog. As if the child had given the table a kick, and gone to sleep.

Charles Dickens,
Our Mutual Friend (1865)

RB.23.b.5212

15 August

The Grandour of London

October 4 1686

Now as to the Grandour of London, Would not England be easier and perhaps stronger if these vitals were more equally dispersed? Is there not a Tumour in that place, and too much matter for mutiny and Terrour to the Government if it should Burst? Is there not too much of our Capital in one stake, liable to the Ravage of Plague and fire? Does not the Assembly too much increase Mortality and lessen Births, and the Church-yards become Infectious? Will not the Resort of the Wealthy and emulation to Luxury, melt down the order of Superiors among and bring all towards Levelling and Republican?

Robert Southwell, letter to Sir William Petty, in Petty Southwell Correspondence, 1676–1687, ed. Marquis of Lansdowne (1928)

010920.cc.9

16 August

A Widely Inhuman Grotesque

Nothing in Moscow is quite like anything one has seen anywhere else; and no two houses, all of which are so unlike the houses in any other country, are quite like one another. Their roofs are almost invariably painted green, and the water-pipes make a sort of green edging around the house-front. But the colours of the houses are endless: green, pink, blue, brown, red, chocolate, lilac, black even, rarely two of the same colour side by side, and rarely two of so much as the same general shape. Every shop has its walls painted over with rude pictures of the goods to be found inside; the draper has his row of clothed dummies, the hatter his pyramid of hats, the greengrocer his vegetables, the wine-seller his many-coloured bottles. Fruit-stalls meet one everywhere, and from the flower-like bouquet of fruits under their cool awnings there is a constant, shifting glow, the yellows and reds of apples, the purple of plums, the green and yellow of melons, and the crisp, black-spotted pink of melons sliced. And in these coloured streets, which in summer flame with the dry heat of a furnace, walk a multitude of coloured figures, brighter than the peasants of a comic opera; and the colours of their shirts and petticoats and handkerchiefs and bodices flame against the sunlight. [...] Russian architecture which seems to proceed from an imaginary assumption to an impossible conclusion, has no standard of beauty to which its caprices of line can appeal, but presents itself rather as a wildly inhuman grotesque, without root in nature or limitation in art.

Arthur Symons, *Cities* (1903)

10106.ff.23

17 August

An Asylum to All: A Prison to None

Never, by force or intimidation, never by prohibition or obstruction, will I use any endeavour to prevent my fellow-countrymen, or any of them, from seeking to better their condition in any other part, inhabited or uninhabited, of this globe. In the territory of this State, I behold an asylum to all: a prison to none.

Jeremy Bentham, *Constitutional Code: For the Use of all Nations, and all Governments Professing Liberal Opinions* (1830)

522.i.14

⚜ 18 August ⚜

The Ideal *of an Italian City*

Of all the places I have seen in Italy, it is the one by far I should most covet to live in. It is the *ideal* of an Italian city, once great, now a shadow of itself. Whichever way you turn, you are struck with picturesque beauty and faded splendours, but with nothing squalid, mean, or vulgar. The grass grows in the well-paved streets. You look down long avenues of buildings, or of garden walls, with summer-houses or fruit-trees projecting over them, and airy palaces with dark portraits gleaming through the grated windows – you turn, and a chapel bounds your view one way, a broken arch another, at the end of the vacant, glimmering, fairy perspective. You are in a dream, in the heart of a romance; you enjoy the most perfect solitude, that of a city which was once filled with 'the busy hum of men,' and of which the tremulous fragments at every step strike the sense, and call up reflection. In short, nothing is to be seen of Ferrara, but the remains, graceful and romantic, of what it was – no sordid object intercepts or sullies the retrospect of the past.

William Hazlitt,
Notes on a Journey through France and Italy (1826)

1049.g.17

❧ 19 August ❧

What Might Be

The large cities of today are scarcely better adapted for the expression of the fraternal spirit than would a work on astronomy which taught that the earth was the centre of the universe be capable of adaptation for use in our schools. Each generation should build to suit its own needs; and it is no more in the nature of things that men should continue to live in old areas because their ancestors lived in them, than it is that they should cherish the old beliefs which a wider faith and a more enlarged understanding have outgrown. The reader is, therefore, earnestly asked not to take it for granted that the large cities in which he may perhaps take a pardonable pride are necessarily, in their present form, any more permanent than the stage coach system which was the subject of so much admiration just at the very moment when it was about to be supplanted by the railways. [...] What Is may hinder What Might Be for a while, but cannot stay the tide or progress. These Crowded cities have done their work; they were the best which a society largely based on selfishness and rapacity could construct, but they are in the nature of things entirely unadapted for a society in which the social side of our nature is demanding a large share of recognition – a society where even the very love of self leads us to insist upon a greater regard for the well-being of our fellows.

Ebenezer Howard, *Garden Cities of Tomorrow* (1902)
W 7/2988

⚹ 20 August ⚹

Merryland

MERRYLAND is a Part of that vast Continent called by the DUTCH Geographers, the *Vroislandtscap*; it is situate in a low Part of the Continent, bounded on the upper Side, or to the Northward, by a little Mountain called MNSVNRS, on the East and West by COXASIN and CODATEXT, and on the south or lower Part it lies open to the TERRA-FIRMA.

There is something very remarkable and surprising as to the *Longitude* and *Latitude* of this Country, neither of which could ever yet be fixed to any certain Degree; and it is pretty evident, however strange it may seem, that there are as great *Variations* both of the Latitude and Longitude in MERRYLAND, as of the Mariner's Compass in other Parts of the World: To confirm this, I beg leave to assure the Reader of a Matter of Fact, which, if he be an entire Stranger to MERRYLAND, he will perhaps scare have Faith to believe; but they who have any tolerable Experience and Knowledge of the Country will be so far from discrediting, that I do not doubt but they will be ready to confirm it by their own Observation.

Roger Pheuquewell [Thomas Stretser],
A New Description of Merryland (5th edn, 1741)
P.C.25.a.65

⚘ 21 August ⚘

The Race of Owner-Occupiers

When Margaret Thatcher initiated the sale of council houses in the 1970s she greatly increased the ratio of housework to time available. Rented accommodation had to be maintained by the landlord, so the tenants did not have to concern themselves with it. Maintenance costs were calculated by the professional landlord as part of an investment that had to bring in a return, and so the costs of improvements to the property were kept to rational levels. The new race of owner-occupiers came into being because they wanted to transform their dwellings into the houses of their dreams and so a new and insidious kind of housework took over. The initial acquisition of the house sucked most people into debt, often more debt than they could service. They then went further into debt to refurbish those houses at a level that the old landlord would have known to be uneconomical. The first thing many of them did was to build an 'extension'; in pubs all over the country men discussed the relative size of their extensions. Once they became owner-occupiers men who had successfully resisted pressure to work *in* the house had no choice but to work *on* the house. Where once the house worked for the owner, the owner worked for the house, endlessly tarting it up, even when the value of the property was steadily declining. The importance of this mechanism in greatly increasing the vulnerability of the workforce can hardly be overstated. Because the indebted worker cannot afford industrial action, the power of the great trade unions was broken, the labour market was restructured, and many members of the brand-new property-owning democracy became unemployed, their houses voracious white elephants. Debt and DIY became a way of life.

Germaine Greer, *The Whole Woman* (1999)

99/22143

22 August

A Rapid Decay of Domestic Affections

January 14, 1801

It appears to me the most calamitous effect, which has followed the measures which have lately been pursued in this country, is a rapid decay of the domestic affections among the lower orders of society. This effect the present Rulers of this Country are not conscious of, or they disregard it. For many years past, the tendency of society amongst almost all the nations of Europe has been to produce it. But recently by the spreading of manufactures through every part of the country, by the heavy taxes upon postage, by workhouses, Houses of Industry, and the invention of Soup-shops &c. superadded to the increasing disproportion between the price of labour and that of the necessaries of life, the bonds of domestic feeling among the poor, as far as the influence of these things has extended, have been weakened, and in innumerable instances entirely destroyed. [...] If it is true, as I believe, that this spirit is rapidly disappearing, no greater curse can befal a land.

William Wordsworth, letter to Charles James Fox, in
The Early Letters of William and Dorothy Wordsworth, 1717–1805,
ed. E. de Selincourt (1935)

010920.k.57

⚜ 23 August ⚜

The Natural Nest of the Human Family

The truth is that the natural nest of the human family is not merely six solid walls, but this box plus a surrounding medium through which sunshine and air can penetrate and in which social activities of vital import to its members can be carried on. When we consider how ruthlessly the city has disrupted the family nest, it is easy to understand the misery peculiar to present urban living.

Clarence Arthur Perry,
Housing for the Machine Age (1939)
352.7 *4936*

24 August

The Little Platoon

To be attached to the subdivision, to love the little platoon
we belong to in society, is the first principle (the germ as
it were) of public affections. It is the first link in the series
by which we proceed towards a love to our country and
to mankind [...] No man ever was attached by a sense of
pride, partiality, or real affection, to a description of
square measurement. He never will glory in belonging to
the Chequer No. 71, or to any other badge-ticket. We begin
our public affections in our families. No cold relation is a
zealous citizen. We pass on to our neighbourhoods and our
habitual provincial connections. These are inns and resting
places. Such divisions of our country as have been forced
by habit and not by a sudden jerk of authority, are so many
little images of that great country in which the heart found
something which it could fill.

Edmund Burke, *Reflections on the Revolution in France* (1790), in
The Works of the Right Honourable Edmund Burke, vol.v (1803)

2500.c.3

25 August

Not a Mere Stagnant Puddle

Parental feeling, as I have experienced it, is very complex. There is, first and foremost, sheer animal affection, and delight in watching what is charming in the ways of the young. Next, there is the sense of inescapable responsibility, providing a purpose for daily activities which scepticism does not easily question. Then there is an egoistic element, which is very dangerous: the hope that one's children may succeed where one has failed, that they may carry on one's work when death or senility puts an end to one's own efforts, and, in any case, that they will supply a biological escape from death, making one's own life part of the whole stream, and not a mere stagnant puddle without any overflow into the future. All this I experienced, and for some years it filled my life with happiness and peace.

Bertrand Russell,
The Autobiography of Bertrand Russell (1967–69; repr. 2009)
YC.2010.a.1285

26 August

A Coyle About My Book

Condemne me not for making such a coyle
About my *Book*, alas it is my *Childe*.
Just like a *Bird*, when her *Young* are in Nest,
Goes in, and out, and hops, and takes no Rest;
But when their *Young* are fledged, their heads out peep,
Lord what a chirping does the *Old* one keep.
So I, for feare my *Strengthlesse Childe* should fall
Against a doore, or stoole, aloud I call,
Bid have a care of such a dangerous place:
Thus write I much, to hinder all *disgrace*.

Margaret Cavendish, Duchess of Newcastle,
'An excuse for so much writ upon my Verses', from *Poems,
and Fancies: Written by the Right Honourable, the Lady Margaret
Countesse of Newcastle* (1653)

79.h.10

27 August

An Orphan Form

Autobiography begins with a sense of being alone. It is an
orphan form.

John Berger, 'Mother', in
Keeping a Rendezvous (1992)
YK.1993.a.2628

28 August

La Necessité

L'esprit n'use de sa faculté créatrice que quand l'expérience lui en impose la necessité.

[The mind uses its faculty for creativity only when experience forces it to do so.]

Henri Poincaré,
La Science et l'Hypothèse (1903)
08464.g.46

29 August

To Wish

1. head
2. green
3. water
4. to sing
5. dead
6. long
7. ship
8. to pay
9. window
10. friendly
11. to cook
12. to ask
13. cold
14. stem
15. to dance
16. village
17. lake
18. sick
19. pride
20. to cook
21. ink
22. angry
23. needle
24. to swim
25. voyage
26. blue
27. lamp
28. to sin
29. bread
30. rich
31. tree
32. to prick
33. pity
34. yellow

35. mountain
36. to die
37. salt
38. new
39. custom
40. to pray
41. money
42. foolish
43. pamphlet
44. despise
45. finger
46. expensive
47. bird
48. to fall
49. book
50. unjust
51. frog
52. to part
53. hunger
54. white
55. child
56. to take care
57. lead pencil
58. sad
59. plum
60. to marry
61. house
62. dear
63. glass
64. to quarrel
65. fur
66. big
67. carrot
68. to paint

69. part
70. old
71. flower
72. to beat
73. box
74. wild
75. family
76. to wish
77. cow
78. friend
79. luck
80. lie
81. deportment
82. narrow
83. brother
84. to fear
85. stork
86. false
87. anxiety
88. to kiss
89. bride
90. pure
91. door
92. to choose
93. hay
94. contented
95. ridicule
96. to sleep
97. month
98. nice
99. woman
100. to abuse

C. G. Jung, 'The Association Method' [1910], in *Collected Papers on Analytical Psychology*, ed. Constance E. Long [1916]

08462.f.18

✼ 30 August ✼

The Wildest Confusion of Receipts

Whoever writes a new book on cookery has to begin with an apology – there are so many, and most of them so bad. All contain good ideas, original or borrowed; but most of them are chaotic and overlaid with rubbish, – the wildest confusion of receipts, distinctions without differences, and endless repetitions, – the result of stupidity, or vanity, and of slavish deference to authority. A trifling variation is given to a well-known dish; a new name is bestowed upon it to flatter somebody's vanity; and then follows another and another receipt to choke up the cookery books and to bewilder their readers. People run after novelties which are not novelties at all, and in the turmoil of details lose sight of the central idea which ought to govern the composition.

E. S. Dallas, *Kettner's Book of the Table:*
A Manual of Cookery: Practical, Theoretical, Historical (1877)

7955.b.41

31 August

My Whole Philosophy

All these different things – is there any limit to what you are prepared to collect?

No. My whole philosophy is that there should be no limit, because otherwise one is limiting the collection. There are some collectors of postcards who will only collect ones that fit into their album. If they get a postcard that won't, because it's a fraction of an inch too big – dammit! You know, they virtually chuck it away because it doesn't conform. It know collectors who collect tins of a certain size because that's all they want to do. They're not really collectors, to my mind, they are just gatherers, people who want to put things up on a mantelpiece to look interesting. I could take you through an analysis which will say, 'There's nothing which I cannot find a reason for saving.'

'An Interview with Robert Opie',
in *The Cultures of Collecting*,
eds John Elsner and Roger Cardinal (1994)

YC.1994.b.5675

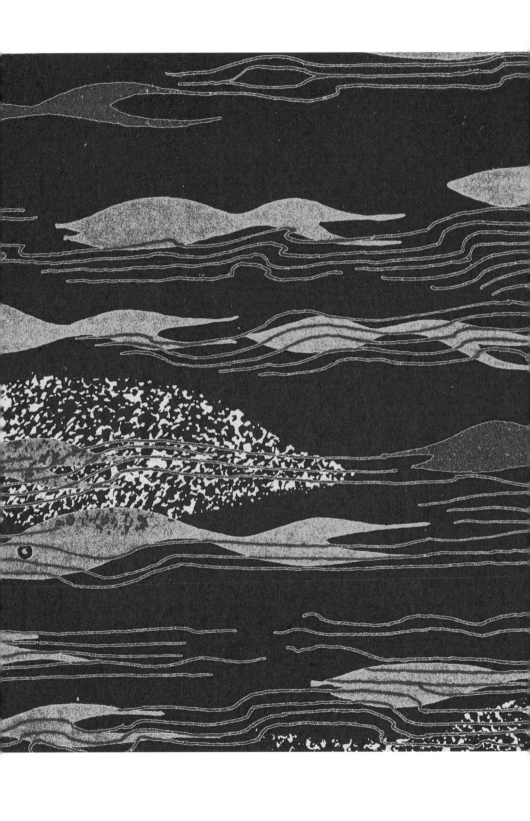

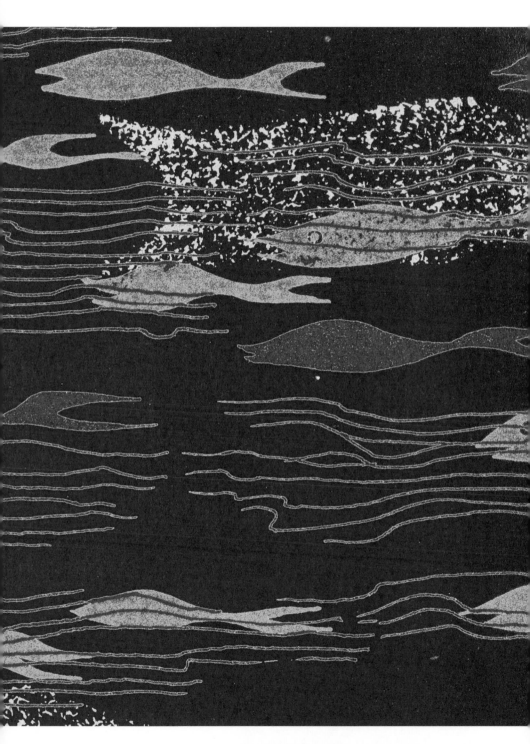

SEPTEMBER

~ 1 September ~

Literary Cooks

He liked those literary cooks
Who skim the cream of others' books;
And ruin half an author's graces
By plucking bon-mots from their places.

Hannah More, *Florio: a tale for fine gentlemen and fine ladies:
and, The Bas Bleu; or, conversation: two poems* (1786; 2nd edn 1787)

11641.g.27

~ 2 September ~

Travail with Expression of Another

De vita humana. – I have considered our whole life is like a
play: wherein every man, forgetful of himself, is in travail
with expression of another. Nay, we so insist in imitating
others, as we cannot, when it is necessary, return to
ourselves; like children that imitate the vices of stammerers
so long, till at last they become such, and make the habit to
another nature, as it is never forgotten.

Ben Jonson, *Timber; or Discoveries made upon men and matter, as
they have flowed out of his daily readings, or had their reflux to his
peculiar notion of the times* [1641]; in *Ben Jonson: Vol. VIII: The Poems,
The Prose Works*, eds C. H. Herford, Percy Simpson,
and Evelyn Simpson (1947)

1482.d.15

⊷ 3 September ⊶

Infallible Ways of Pleasing an Author

There are three infallible ways of pleasing an author, and the three form a rising scale of compliment: 1 – to tell him you have read one of his books; 2 – to tell him you had read all of his books; 3 – to ask him to let you read the manuscript of his forthcoming book. No.1 admits you to his respect; No. 2 admits you to his admiration; No. 3 carries you clear into his heart.

Mark Twain, *Pudd'nhead Wilson* (1894)
X27/3270

⊷ 4 September ⊶

Not a Man as Folks Could Crack Wi'

'Was he,' I said, 'a sociable man, Mr. Wordsworth, in the earliest times you can remember?'
    'Wudsworth [...] He was not a man as folks could crack wi', nor not a man as could crack wi' folks.'

Canon H. D. Rawnsley, 'Reminiscences of Wordsworth Among the Peasantry of Westmoreland' (1882), in *Worsworthiana: A Selection of Papers Read to the Wordsworth Society*, ed. William Angus Knight (1889)
011840.e.33

➤ 5 September ➤

My Mouth is Out of Tast

Ever myn happe is slack and slo in commyng,
    Desir encresing, myn hope uncertain,
    That leve it or wayt it doeth me like pain,
    And Tigre like, swift it is in parting.
Alas, the snow shalbe black and scalding,
    The See waterles, fisshe in the moyntain,
    The Tamys shall retorne back into his fountain,
    And where he rose the sonne shall take lodging,
Ere that I in this fynde peace or quyetenes,
    Or that love or my lady rightwisely
    Leve to conspire again me wrongfully;
And if that I have after suche bitternes
    Any thing swete, my mouth is owte of tast,
    That all my trust and travaill is but wast.

Thomas Wyatt, in *Tottel's Miscellany: Songes and Sonettes
by Henry Howard, Earl of Surrey, Sir Thomas Wyatt, the Elder,
Nicolas Grimald, and uncertain authors* (1557; 1870)

01221.c.2/24

⤚ 6 September ⤜

Knowing What to Neglect

If a writer will go on the principle of stopping everywhere and anywhere to put down his notes, as the true painter will stop anywhere and everywhere to sketch, he will be able to cut down his works liberally. He will become prodigal not of writing – any fool can be this – but of omission. You become brief because you have more things to say than time to say them in. One of the chief arts is that of knowing what to neglect.

Samuel Butler,
The Notebooks, ed. Henry Festing Jones (1912)
828.8 *4564*

⤚ 7 September ⤜

Noah Was a Genius

Noah had three sons, Shem, Ham, and Japheth. Ham only noticed that his father was a drunkard, and completely lost sight of the fact that he was genius, that he had built an ark and saved the world.

Anton Chekhov, *Letters of Anton Tchehov to his Family and Friends*, trans. Constance Garnett (1920)
010905.h.31

～ 8 September ～

The Government of Yahoos

My design was, if possible, to discover some small island uninhabited, yet sufficient by my labour to furnish me with the necessaries of life, which I would have thought a greater happiness than to be first minister in the politest court in Europe; so horrible was the idea I conceived of returning to live in the society and under the government of yahoos.

Lemuel Gulliver [Jonathan Swift],
Travels into Several Remote Nations of the World (1726)
Ashley 1828

➤ 9 September ➤

Degraded Victims of Fate

Imagine the most insignificant, the most cowardly creature, an outcast from society, of no service to anyone, utterly useless, utterly disgusting, but incredibly vain, though entirely destitute of any talent by which he might have justified his morbidly sensitive vanity. I hasten to add that Foma Fomitch was the incarnation of unbounded vanity, but that at the same time it was a special kind of vanity – that is, the vanity found in a complete nonentity, and, as is usual in such cases, a vanity mortified and oppressed by grievous failures in the past; a vanity that has begun rankling long, long ago, and ever since has given off envy and venom, at every encounter, at every success of anyone else. I need hardly say that all this was seasoned with the most unseemly touchiness, the most insane suspiciousness. It may be asked, how is one to account for such vanity? How does it arise, in spite of complete insignificance, in pitiful creatures who are forced by their social position to know their place? How answer such a question? Who knows, perhaps, there are exceptions of whom my hero is one? He certainly is an exception to the rule, as will be explained later. But allow me to ask: are you certain that those who are completely resigned to be your buffoons, your parasites and your toadies, and consider it an honour and a happiness to be so, are you certain that they are quite devoid of vanity and envy? What of the slander and backbiting and tale-bearing and mysterious whisperings in back corners, somewhere aside and at your table? Who knows, perhaps, in some of these degraded victims of fate, your fools and buffoons, vanity far from being dispelled by humiliation is even aggravated by that very humiliation, by being a fool and buffoon, by eating the bread of dependence and being for ever forced to submission and self-suppression? Who knows, maybe, this ugly exaggerated vanity is only a false fundamentally depraved sense of personal dignity, first outraged, perhaps, in childhood by oppression, poverty, filth, spat upon, perhaps, in the person of the future outcast's parents before his eyes?

Fyodor Dostoevsky, *The Friend of the Family*,
trans. Constance Garnett (1920)

X15/2307

❧ 10 September ❧

A Necessary Obstacle

The first relationship is not with objects but with obstacles. Or to put it another way, from the other end, so to speak: people fall in love at the moments in their lives when they are most terrorized by possibilities. In order to fall in love with someone they must be perceived to be an obstacle, a necessary obstacle.

Adam Phillips, *On Kissing, Tickling and Being Bored: psychoanalytic essays on the unexamined life* (1993)

93/08004

❧ 11 September ❧

A Horror of Inscrutable Shadow

In the room of one of my friends hangs a mirror. It is an oblong sheet of glass, set in a frame of dark, highly varnished wood, carved in the worst taste of the Regency period, and relieved with faded gilt. Glancing at it from a distance you would guess the thing a relic from some 'genteel' drawing-room of Miss Austen's time. But go nearer and look into the glass itself. By some malformation or mere freak of make, all the images it throws back are livid. Flood the room with sunshine; stand before this glass with youth and hot blood tingling on your cheeks; and the glass will give back neither sun nor colour; but your own face, blue and dead, and behind it a horror of inscrutable shadow.

Q [Sir Arthur Quiller-Couch], 'A Dark Mirror', in *Noughts and Crosses: Stories, Studies and Sketches* (1897)

012357.f.11

⤙ 12 September ⤚

The Order of Civilization is Reversed Here

I was a slave – born a slave – and though the fact was incomprehensible to me, it conveyed to my mind a sense of my entire dependence on the will of somebody I had never seen; and, from some cause or other, I had been made to fear this somebody above all else on earth. [...] Slavery does away with fathers, as it does away with families. Slavery has no use for either fathers or families, and its laws do not recognize their existence in the social arrangements of the plantation. When they *do* exist, they are not the outgrowths of slavery, but are antagonistic to that system. The order of civilization is reversed here. [...] There is not, beneath the sky, an enemy to filial affection so destructive as slavery. It had made my brothers and sisters strangers to me; it converted the mother that bore me, into a myth; it shrouded my father in mystery, and left me without an intelligible beginning in the world.

Frederick Douglass,
My Bondage and My Freedom (1855)

10880.bb.9

⊷ 13 September ⊷

Thy Genial Rays to Parts Confined

If Heaven has into being deigned to call
Thy light, O LIBERTY! to shine on all;
Bright intellectual Sun! why does thy ray
To earth distribute only partial day?
Since no resisting cause from *spirit* flows
Thy universal presence to oppose;
No obstacles by Nature's hand impress'd,
Thy subtle and ethereal beams arrest;
Not swayed by *matter* is thy course benign,
Or more direct or more oblique to shine;
Nor motion's laws can speed thy active course;
Nor strong repulsion's pow'rs obstruct thy force:
Since there is no convexity in MIND,
Why are thy genial rays to parts confined?
While the chill North with thy bright beam is blest,
Why should fell darkness half the South invest?
Was it decreed, fair Freedom! at thy birth,
That thou should'st ne'er irradiate *all* the earth?
While Britain basks in thy full blaze of light,
Why lies sad Afric quench'd in total night?

Hannah More,
from *Slavery: A Poem* (1788)

840.l.14.(8.)

⚔ 14 September ⚔

The World in a Pretty Pass

The old century is very nearly out, and leaves the world in a pretty pass, and the British Empire is playing the devil in it as never an empire before on so large a scale. We may live to see its fall. All the nations of Europe are making the same hell upon earth in China, massacring and pillaging and raping in the captured cities as outrageously as in the Middle Ages. The Emperor of Germany gives the word for slaughter and the Pope looks on and approves. In South Africa our troops are burning farms under Kitchener's command, and the Queen and the two houses of Parliament, and the bench of bishops thank God publicly and vote money for the work. The Americans are spending fifty millions a year on slaughtering the Filipinos; the King of the Belgians has invested his whole fortune on the Congo, where he is brutalizing the negroes to fill his pockets. The French and Italians for the moment are playing a less prominent part in the slaughter, but their inactivity grieves them. The whole white race is revelling openly in violence, as though it had never pretended to be Christian. God's equal curse be on them all! So ends the famous nineteenth century into which we were so proud to have been born. [...]

31st Dec. 1900.

I bid good-bye to the old century, may it rest in peace as it has lived in war. Of the new century I prophesy nothing except that it will see the decline of the British Empire. Other worse empires will rise perhaps in its place, but I shall not live to see the day. It all seems a very little matter here in Egypt, with the pyramids watching us as they watched Joseph, when, as a young man four thousand years ago, perhaps in this very garden, he walked and gazed at the sunset behind them, wondering about the future just as I did this evening. And so, poor wicked nineteenth century, farewell!

Wilfrid Scawen Blunt, *My Diaries: A Personal Narrative of Events, 1888–1914* (1922)

920 *413*

⤫ 15 September ⤫

The Establishment of a Genuine Democracy

Analysis of Imperialism, with its natural supports, militarism, oligarchy, bureaucracy, protection, concentration of capital and violent trade fluctuations, has marked it out as the supreme danger of modern national States. The power of the imperialist forces within the nation to use the national resources for their private gain, by operating the instrument of the State, can only be overthrown by the establishment of a genuine democracy, the direction of public policy by the people for the people through representatives over whom they exercise a real control.

J. A. Hobson, *Imperialism: A Study* (1902)
8155.cc.12

⤫ 16 September ⤫

When These Things Can Be Said

When it shall be said in any country in the world, My poor are happy; neither ignorance nor distress is to be found among them; my jails are empty of prisoners, my streets of beggars; the aged are not in want; the taxes are not oppressive; the rational world is my friend, because I am the friend of happiness: When these things can be said, then may that country boast its Constitution and its Government.

Thomas Paine, *Rights of Man* (1792),
ed. Hypatia Bradlaugh Bonner (1985)
W81/3406

⫷ 17 September ⫸

The Mad and Insatiable Ambition of Princes

The very idea of distant possessions will be even ridiculed. The East and West Indies, and everything without ourselves will be disregarded, and wholly excluded from all European systems; and only those divisions of men, and of territory, will take place which the common convenience requires, and not such as the mad and insatiable ambition of princes demands. No part of America, Africa, or Asia, will be held in subjection to any part of Europe, and all the intercourse that will be kept up among them will be for their mutual advantage.

Joseph Priestley, *Letters to the Right Honourable Edmund Burke, occasioned by his Reflections on the Revolution in France, &c.* (1791), repr. in *The Theological and Miscellaneous works of Joseph Priestley*, vol.22 (1828)

W68/663o

➤ 18 September ➤

Life in the Future

The Communist way of life will not form itself blindly, like coral islands, but will be built consciously, will be tested by thought, will be directed and corrected. Life will cease to be elemental and, for this reason, stagnant. Man will learn to move rivers and mountains, to build peoples' palaces on the peaks of Mont Blanc and at the bottom of the Atlantic; and he will not only be able to impart richness, brilliancy, and intensity to his life but also the highest dynamic quality. The shell of life will hardly have time to form before it will be burst open again under the pressure of new technical and cultural inventions and achievements. Life in the future will not be monotonous.

Leon Trotsky, *Literature and Revolution*,
trans. Rose Strunsky (1925)

011840.aa.17

➤ 19 September ➤

Not Possible to Refuse

Politics in a work of literature are like a pistol-shot in the middle of a concert, something loud and vulgar and yet a thing to which it is not possible to refuse one's attention.

Stendhal, *The Charterhouse of Parma* [1839],
trans. C. K. Scott Moncrieff (1926)

012591.n.1

⤚ 20 September ⤛

The True Ideal of a Full and Reasonable Life

To sum up, then, the study of history and the love and practice of art forced me into a hatred of the civilisation which, if things were to stop as they are, would turn history into inconsequent nonsense, and make art a collection of the curiosities of the past which would have no serious relation to the life of the present.

But the consciousness of revolution stirred amidst our hateful modern society prevented me, luckier than many others of artistic perceptions, from crystallizing into a mere railer against 'progress' on the one hand, and on the other from wasting time and energy in any of the numerous schemes by which the quasi-artistic of the middle classes hope to make art grow when it has no longer any root, and thus I became a practical Socialist. [...] It is the province of art to set the true ideal of a full and reasonable life before him, a life to which the perception and creation of beauty, the enjoyment of real pleasure that is, shall be felt to be as necessary to man as his daily bread, and that no man, and no set of men, can be deprived of this except by mere opposition, which should be resisted to the utmost.

William Morris, 'How I Became a Socialist' (1894), in *Collected Works*, ed. May Morris, vol. XXIII (1915)

W 9/245i

21 September

Good People

Good people are the very devil sometimes, because, when their goodwill hits on a wrong way, they go much further along it and are much more ruthless than bad people; but there is always hope in the fact that they mean well, and that their bad deeds are their mistakes and not their successes; whereas the evils done by bad people are not mistakes but triumphs of wickedness. And since all moral triumphs, like mechanical triumphs, are reached by trial and error, we can despair of Democracy and despair of Capitalism without despairing of human nature: indeed if we did not despair of them as we know them we should prove ourselves so worthless that there would be nothing left for the world but to wait for the creation of a new race of beings capable of succeeding where we have failed.

George Bernard Shaw,
The Intelligent Woman's Guide to Socialism and Capitalism (1928)
08286.c.32

22 September

It is Not Benevolence

It is not from the benevolence of the butcher, the brewer, or the baker that we expect our dinner, but from their regard to their own interest. We address ourselves, not to their humanity but to their self-love, and never talk to them of our own necessities but of their advantages.

Adam Smith,
An Inquiry into the nature and causes of the Wealth of Nations (1776)
31.e.9-10

~ 23 September ~

Rules

XIV

There are two great rules of life, the one general and the other particular. The first is that every one can, in the end, get what he wants if he only tries. This is the general rule. The particular rule is that every individual is, more or less, an exception to the general rule.

XV

Nature is essentially mean, mediocre. You can have schemes for raising the level of this mean, but not for making every one two inches taller than his neighbour, and this is what people really care about.

XVI

All progress is based upon a universal innate desire on the part of every organism to live beyond its income.

Samuel Butler, *The Note-Books of Samuel Butler*,
ed. Henry Festing Jones (1912)
828.8 *4576*

⤞ 24 September ⤝

Good Breeding

Good breeding consists in concealing how much we think of ourselves and how little we think of others.

Mark Twain, *Mark Twain's Notebooks: journals, letters, observations, wit, wisdom, and doodles*, ed. Carlo DeVito (2015)
ELD.DS.25636

⤞ 25 September ⤝

The Secret of Self-Confidence

Life for both sexes is arduous, difficult, a perpetual struggle. It calls for gigantic courage and strength. More than anything, perhaps, creatures of illusion as we are, it calls for confidence in oneself. Without self-confidence we are babes in the cradle. And how can we generate this imponderable quality, which is yet so invaluable, most quickly? By thinking that other people are inferior to oneself.

Virginia Woolf, *A Room of One's Own* (1929)
W18/0533

⟊ 26 September ⟊

Branded on the Tongue

The great majority of people can still be 'placed' in an instant by their manners, clothes, and general appearance. Even the physical type differs considerably, the upper classes being on average several inches taller than the working class. But the most striking difference of all is in language and accent. The English working class, as Mr. Wyndham Lewis has put it, are 'branded on the tongue'.

George Orwell, *The English People* (1947)
W.P.10933/1.(96.)

⇜ 27 September ⇝

Vulgar to Someone

All of us seem vulgar to someone.

Louis MacNeice, 'In Defence of Vulgarity' (1937),
repr. in *Selected Prose of Louis MacNeice*,
ed. Alan Heuser (1990)
YC.1990.a.6682

✦ 28 September ✦

His Majestic Torrent

I am aware that many will say I have not spoken highly enough of Dr. Johnson; but it will be difficult for those who say so to speak more highly. If I have described his manners as they were, I have been careful to show his superiority to the common forms of common life. It is surely no dispraise to an oak that it does not bear jessamine; and he who should plant honeysuckle round Trajan's column would not be thought to adorn, but to disgrace it.

When I have said that he was more a man of genius than of learning, I mean not to take from the one part of his character that which I willingly give to the other. The erudition of Mr. Johnson proved his genius; for he had not acquired it by long or profound study: nor can I think those characters the greatest which have most learning driven into their heads, any more than I can persuade myself to consider the River Jenisca as superior to the Nile, because the first receives near seventy tributary streams in the course of its unmarked progress to the sea, while the great parent of African plenty, flowing from an almost invisible source, and unenriched by any extraneous waters, except eleven nameless rivers, pours his majestic torrent into the ocean by seven celebrated mouths.

Hesther Lynch Piozzi, *Anecdotes of the late Samuel Johnson, LL.D. during the last twenty years of his life* (1786; 1925 edn)

X29/2802

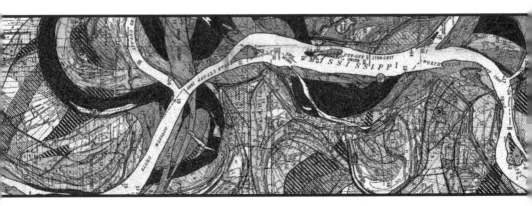

➤ 29 September ➤

From Nature for Nothing

January 7 1889

What writers belonging to the upper class have received from nature for nothing, plebians acquire at the cost of their youth. Write a story of how a young man, the son of a serf, who has served in a shop, sung in a choir, been at a high school and a university, who has been brought up to respect everyone of higher rank and position, to kiss priests' hands, to reverence other people's ideas, to be thankful for every morsel of bread, who has been many times whipped, who has trudged from one pupil to another without galoshes, who has been used to fighting, and tormenting animals, who has liked dining with his rich relations, and been hypocritical before God and men from the mere consciousness of his own insignificance – write how this young man squeezes the slave out of himself, drop by drop, and how waking one beautiful morning he feels that he has no longer a slave's blood in his veins but a real man's…

Anton Chekhov, *Letters of Anton Tchehov to his Family and Friends*, trans. Constance Garnett (1920)

010905.h.31

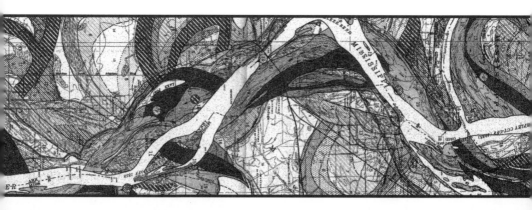

Die Zauberer, Alchimisten, Astrologen und Hexen

Glaubt ihr denn, daß die Wissenschaften entstanden und
groß geworden wären, wenn ihnen nicht die Zauberer,
Alchimisten, Astrologen und Hexen vorangelaufen wären
als die, welche mit ihren Verheißungen und Vorspiegelungen
erst Durst, Hunger und Wohlgeschmack an verborgenen
und verbotenen Mächten schaffen mußten?

(Do you believe then the sciences would ever have arisen and
become great if there had not beforehand been magicians,
alchemists, astrologers and wizards, who thirsted and
hungered after abscondite and forbidden powers?)

Friedrich Nietzsche,
Die fröhliche Wissenschaft (1886)
8467.f.39

OCTOBER

 1 October

The Finer and Better Things of Life

I have known the tremendous exaltation of victory in the ring, in love, in business and in controversies of all kinds, and I have been cast down into the despair that sometimes comes with failure. I have traveled in nearly every country of the world and wherever I have gone I have had adventures that men of my race and nation have never had. [...] The possession of muscular strength and the courage to use it in contests with other men for physical supremacy does not necessarily imply a lack of appreciation for the finer and better things of life. Brutish qualities and base inclinations are prevalent in all classes. A man's vocation is no measure of his inner feelings nor a guarantee of his earnest desire to live right and attain the highest standards.

Jack Johnson,
Jack Johnson In the Ring – and Out (1927)
010884.de.26

 2 October

Success is to be Measured

Success is to be measured not so much by the position that one has reached in life as by the obstacles which he has overcome while trying to succeed.

Booker T. Washington,
Up from Slavery: An Autobiography (1901; 1902 edn)
10880.c.38

 3 October

To Avoid Corners Altogether

The unexpectedness of life, waiting round every corner, catches even wise women unawares. To avoid corners altogether is, after all, to refuse to live. But most people learn by experience what may be coming; they keep themselves elastic, so as to swerve a little to left or right if an obstacle appears, and adapt their contours in some degree to the asperities of the surrounding world. My mother never thought of doing this. It was no strength in her, for she was uncertain of her direction and inclined to adopt the most promiscuous guidance as it came: but she could not realise that the object in the middle of her path was an obstacle, and would throw herself against it as I have seen horses (unreasonable animals) fling themselves against a van or doorway when blinded by some fright or fancy of their own. Just so, and with the same reaction or baffled injury, my mother flung herself against the adverse facts of life, and never I think, to the end of her days, understood how easy it would have been to circumvent them.

Freya Stark,
Traveller's Prelude (1950)
10862.c.23

❋ 4 October ❋

An Innate Inability of Mutual Comprehension

I was told that the Privileged and the People formed Two
Nations, governed by different laws, influenced by different
manners, with no thoughts or sympathies in common; with
an innate inability of mutual comprehension.

Benjamin Disraeli, *Sybil; Or, The Two Nations* (1845)
12651.ff.32

❋ 5 October ❋

We Are The Many

We are the many who served the few;
We made their glory, and strength, and gain;
We passed as sand, when the west wind blew,
As the myriad drops of the autumn rain;

We sank at night off the surge-beat strand, –
The rotting bark and its living freight,
The o'erflowing swarm of a straitened land,
Who went forth bravely to seek their fate.
[...]
We are the souls who were pent within
The narrow street and the valley dim;
Bred in the darkness of want and sin,
We peopled the hulks and the prisons grim.
[...]

Ye lack emotions who live at ease
In bright warm chambers of prosp'rous life;
Ye tales of terror and sorrow please –
Look out around ye, they're rife, aye, – rife,

As berries in autumn, as leaves in May,
Seek! ye will find in the neighbouring street
Tragedies acted before the day,
That stir the heart to a quicker beat,
And draw the tear from its deepest seat.

Henrietta Tindal, *Lines and Leaves* (1850?)
11645.a.33

 6 October

A Black Mamba

A man of my sorts, who has travelled about the world in rough places, gets on perfectly well with two classes, what you may call the upper and the lower. He understands them and they understand him. I was at home with herds and tramps and roadmap, and I was sufficiently at my ease with people like Sir Walter and the men I had met the night before. I can't explain why, but it is a fact. But what fellows like me don't understand is the great comfortable, satisfied middle-class world, the folk that live in villas and suburbs. He doesn't know how they look at things, he doesn't understand their conventions, and he is as shy of them as of a black mamba.

John Buchan, *The Thirty-Nine Steps* (1915)
12601.ccc.25

7 October

The Partnership Principle

Finally, I must repeat my conviction, that the industrial economy which divides society absolutely into two portions, the payers of wages and the receivers of them, the first counted by thousands and the last by millions, is neither fit for, nor capable of, indefinite duration: and the possibility of changing this system for one of combination without dependence, and unity of interest instead of organized hostility, depends altogether upon the future developments of the Partnership principle.

John Stuart Mill, *Principles of Political Economy* (1848),
ed. W. J. Ashley (1917)

330 *1579*

8 October

A Small Manufactory

One man draws out the wire, another straights it, a third cuts it, a fourth points, a fifth grinds it at the top for receiving the head; to make the head requires two or three distinct operations; to put it on is a peculiar business, to whiten the pin is another [...] I have seen a small manufactory where ten men only were employed [...] though they were very poor and therefore but indifferently accommodated with the necessary machinery, those ten persons could make among them upwards of forty-eight thousand pins in a day [...] But if they had all wrought separately and independently [...] they certainly could not each of them have made twenty, perhaps not one pin in a day.

Adam Smith, *An Inquiry into the Nature and Causes
of the Wealth of Nations* (1776)

31.e.9-10

9 October

A Cant Abroad

There is a cant abroad at the present day, that there is a special pleasure in industry, and hence we are taught to regard all those who object to work as appertaining to the class of natural vagabonds; but where is the man among us who loves labour? For work or labour is merely that which is irksome to perform and which every man requires a certain remuneration to induce him to perform. If men really loved work they would pay to be allowed to do it rather than require to be paid for doing it.

Henry Mayhew,
London Labour and the London Poor (1861–62)

08275.bb.28

10 October

On a Level with Dentists

If economists could get themselves thought of as humble, competent people, on a level with dentists, that would be splendid!

John Maynard Keynes,
Essays in Persuasion (1931)

W8/4351

 11 October

Dollars Damn Me

In a week or so, I go to New York, to bury myself in a third-story room and work and slave only 'whale' while it is driving through the press. *That* is the only way I can finish it now, – I am so pulled hither and thither by circumstances. The calm, the coolness, the silent grass-growing mood in which a man *ought* always to compose, – that, I fear, can never be mine. Dollars damn me; and the malicious Devil is forever grinning upon me, holding the door ajar. My dear Sir, a presentiment is upon me, – I shall at last be worn out and perish, like an old nutmeg-grater, grated to pieces by the constant attrition of the wood, that is, the nutmeg. What I feel the most moved to write, that is banned, – it will not pay. So the product is a final hash, and all my books are botches.

Herman Melville, letter to Nathaniel Hawthorne, June 1851,
q. in *Nathaniel Hawthorne and His Wife, A Biography*,
Julian Hawthorne, vol.1 (1885)

10882.d.8

✳ 12 October ✳

Fretted, Disappointed, and Ruined

You will come here; you will observe what the artists are doing; and you will sometimes speak a disapprobation in plain words, and sometimes by a no less expressive silence. By degrees you will produce some of your own works. They will be variously criticized; you will defend them; you will abuse those that have attacked you; expostulations, discussions, letters, possibly challenges, will go forward; you will shun your brethren, they will shun you. In the meantime, gentlemen will avoid your friendship, for fear of being engaged in your quarrels; you will fall into distresses which will only aggravate your disposition for further quarrels; you will be obliged for maintenance to do anything for anybody; your very talents will depart for want of hope and encouragement; and you will go out of the world fretted, disappointed, and ruined.

Edmund Burke, letter to James Barry, 16 September 1769, in *The Works of James Barry* (1809)

561*.d.9

 13 October

Trivial Controversies

There is nothing which is not the subject of debate, and in which men of learning are not of contrary opinions. The most trivial question escapes not our controversy, and in the most momentous we are not able to give any certain decision. Disputes are multiplied as if everything was uncertain.

David Hume, *A Treatise of Human Nature* (1745)
C.175.c.8.(2.)

 14 October

No Good in Discussion

He was no good in discussion, not because any amount of argument could shake his faith, but because the mere fact of hearing another voice disconcerted him painfully, confusing his thoughts at once – these thoughts that for so many years, in a mental solitude more barren than a waterless desert, no living voice had ever combated, commented, or approved.

Joseph Conrad, *The Secret Agent* (1907)
012626.aaa.30

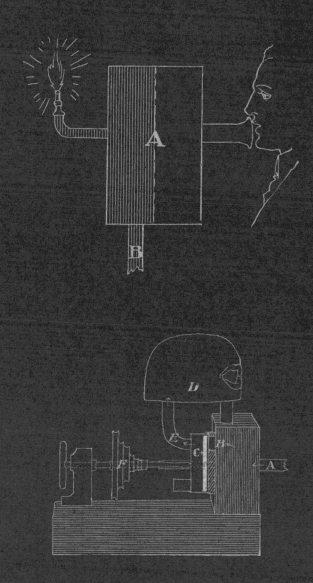

 15 October

This Mill

He appears to me like a great mill, into which a subject is thrown to be ground. It requires, indeed, fertile minds to furnish materials for this mill. I regret whenever I see it unemployed; but sometimes I feel myself quite barren, and having nothing to throw in.

James Boswell, *The Journal of a Tour to the Hebrides with Samuel Johnson* (1785)

567.c.16

16 October

Other Hands Than Mine

Experience has shown me that with several hundred men performing daily a multitude of acts of greater or lesser importance, a certain uniformity of method is necessary to lighten their own labour and the labour of those to whom is entrusted the auditing of their accounts and returns. Such subjects as the advisability of uniform filing of paper or folding of returns, of using dots instead of o's in money columns, or of forwarding returns at the earliest instead of the latest date allowable, may seem to trivial to treat of; yet every Clerk would do well to remember that a rigid adherence to the advice on such matters which I have given would facilitate the audit of the returns almost in the measure of the services of a Clerk in Registrar's office. [...] My part has been to formulate a Code by the collecting and the collating of an immense mass of materials, the major part of which, having been once carefully examined, need never be referred to again. The perfecting of the work will be aided by those who systematise and record their experience, and must rest with other hands than mine.

Bram Stoker, *The Duties of Clerks of Petty Sessions in Ireland* (1879)

C.S.A.26/19

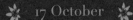 17 October

My Whole Circumambient Universe

If we think about it, we find that our life *consists* in this achieving of a pure relationship between ourselves and the living universe about us. This is how I 'save my soul' by accomplishing a pure relationship between me and another person, me and other people, me and a nation, me and a race of men, me and the animals, me and the trees or flowers, me and the earth, me and the skies and sun and stars, me and the moon: an infinity of pure relations, big and little like the stars of the sky: that makes our eternity, for each one of us, me and the timber I am sawing, the lines of force I follow; me and the dough I knead for bread, me and the very motion with which I write, me and the bit of gold I have got. This, if we knew it, is our life and our eternity: the subtle perfected relation between me and my whole circumambient universe.

D. H. Lawrence, 'Morality and the Novel' (1925),
in *Phoenix: The Posthumous Papers of D. H. Lawrence*
(1936)

824.9 *4747*

 18 October

The Web, Then

The web, then, or the pattern; a web at once sensuous and logical, an elegant and pregnant texture: that is style, that is the foundation of the art of literature.

Robert Louis Stevenson,
'On Some Technical Elements of
Style in Literature' (1885),
in *Essays in the Art of Writing* (1919)

801 *5236*

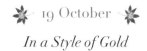 19 October

In a Style of Gold

I AM the Empire in the last of its decline,
That sees the tall, fair-haired Barbarians pass, –
the while
Composing indolent acrostics, in a style
Of gold, with languid sunshine dancing in each line.

Paul Verlaine, 'Langueur', in *Poems*,
trans. Gertrude Hall (1895)

011483.e.1

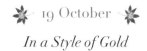 20 October

A Bright Piece of that Late Afternoon Sun

What can you do if you are thirty and, turning the corner of
your own street, you are overcome, suddenly by a feeling of
bliss – absolute bliss! – as though you'd suddenly swallowed
a bright piece of that late afternoon sun and it burned in
your bosom, sending out a little shower of sparks into every
particle, into every finger and toe?

Katherine Mansfield, 'Bliss' (1918),
in *Bliss and Other Stories* (1920)

NN.6731

 21 October

To Paint the Summer Morning

Who has not waked to list the busy sounds
Of summer morning in the sultry smoke
Of noisy London? On the pavement hot
The sooty chimney-boy, with dingy face
And tattered covering, shrilly bawls his trade,
Rousing the sleepy housemaid. At the door
The milk-pail rattles, and the tinkling bell
Proclaims the dustman's office, while the street
Is lost in clouds imperious. Now begins
The din of hackney carriages, wagons, carts;
While tin men's shops, and noisy trunk-makers,
Knife-grinders, coopers, squeaking cork-cutters,
Fruit-barrows, and the hunger-giving cries
Of vegetable vendors, fill the air.
[...] All along
The sultry pavement, the old-clothes man cries
In tone monotonous, and sidelong views
The area for his traffic. Now the bag
Is slily opened, and the half-worn suit
(Sometimes the pilfered treasures of the base
Domestic spoiler) for one half its worth
Sinks in the green abyss. The porter now
Bears his huge load along the burning way,
And the poor poet wakes from busy dreams
To paint the summer morning.

Mary Robinson, from 'A London Summer Morning',
in *The Wild Wreath* (1804)

11642.bbb.55

 22 October

The Whole, Full, Flirtatious Span of It

The past is an empty café terrace.
An airless dusk before thunder. A man running.
And no way now to know what happened then –
none at all – unless, of course, you improvise:

The blackbird on this first sultry morning,
in summer, finding buds, worms, fruit,
feels the heat. Suddenly she puts out her wing –
the whole, full, flirtatious span of it.

Eavan Boland, from
'The Black Lace Fan my Mother Gave me',
in *Outside History* (1990)
YC.1990.a.10112

 23 October

The Happiest Part of a Man's Life

The happiest part of a man's life is what he passes lying awake
in bed in the morning.

James Boswell,
The Journal of a Tour to the Hebrides with Samuel Johnson (1785)
567.c.16

 24 October

The Great Promise of Our Post-Prozac World

We now march off into the next millennium knowing that we will become better, we must become better, we shall become better. We can change our bodies and our lives. We will fit ourselves into society by restructuring our bodies to make our souls happy. We imagine the world outside of ourselves as a happier place than our inner world. For the acquisition (not merely the pursuit) of happiness – or at least the absence of sadness – is the great promise of our post-Prozac world. Aesthetic surgery is one of the means by which we believe we can accomplish this goal.

Happiness in our modern world is in part defined by the desire to vanish into the world beyond ourselves where there is no difference. We want to become happy like everyone else and thus be absolutely unique in our happiness. This contradiction is at the heart of the matter (which is the phrase Sigmund Freud scribbled in the margins of his books when he believed he had found the central truth in his reading). The heart of the matter in aesthetic surgery is the common human desire to 'pass.'

'Passing' is the other side of the coin of our persistent and constant need to generate stereotypes in order to organize the world.

Sander Gilman, *Making the Body Beautiful: A Cultural History of Aesthetic Surgery* (1999)
YC.2002.a.13503

 25 October

Look At This Little Chin of Mine

'Don't you wish you were a woman, Waldo?'

'No,' he answered readily.

'I thought not … I never met a man who did … It is delightful to be a woman; but every man thanks the Lord devoutly that he isn't one. [...] This one thought stands – never goes – if I might but be one of those born in the future; then, perhaps, to be born a woman will not be to be born branded [...] It is not what is done to us, but what is made of us, what wrongs us. No man can be really injured but by what modifies himself. We all enter the world little plastic beings, with so much natural force, perhaps, but for the rest – blank, and the world tells us what we are to be, and shapes us by the ends it sets before us. To you it says – *Work*; and to us it says – *Seem!* To you it says – As you approximate to man's highest ideal of God, as your arm is strong and your knowledge great, and the power to labour is with you, so you shall gain all that human heart desires. To us it says – Strength shall not help you, nor knowledge, nor labour. You shall gain what men gain, but by other means. And so the world makes men and women.'

'Look at this little chin of mine, with the dimple in it. It is but a small part of my person; but though I had a knowledge of all things under the sun, and the wisdom to use it, and the deep loving heart of an angel, it would not stead me through life like this little chin. I can win money with it, I can win love; I can win power with it, I can win fame. What would knowledge help me?'

Olive Schreiner (as 'Ralph Iron'),
The Story of an African Farm (1883)

C.194.a.792

26 October

The Most Essentially Womanly in the World

All men whose opinion is worth having prefer the simple and genuine girl of the past, with her tender little ways and pretty bashful modesties, to this loud and rampant modernisation, with her false red hair and painted skin, talking slang as glibly as a man, and by preference leading the conversation to doubtful subjects. She thinks she is piquant and exciting when she thus makes herself the bad copy of a worse original; and she will not see that though men laugh with her they do not respect her, though they flirt with her they do not marry her; she will not believe that she is not the kind of thing they want, and that she is acting against nature and her own interests when she disregards their advice and offends their taste. We do not understand how she makes out her account, viewing her life from any side; but all we can do is to wait patiently until the national madness has passed, and our women have come back again to the old English ideal, once the most beautiful, the most modest, the most essentially womanly in the world.

Eliza Lynn Lynton, *The Girl of the Period
and Other Social Essays,* vol.1 (1883)

X27/4551

27 October

I Throw the Book From Me In Disgust

Those who read many romances are, I imagine, insensible to the inconsistencies which I am unfortunate enough to detect, even in works written by men of talents and genius; and thus I am deprived of that interest in the perusal of them, which others enjoy to an intense degree. Sometimes I notice incongruities that the most accommodating and indulgent critic would be at a loss to reconcile: sometimes I read a picturesque that turns nature into a second state of chaos; and sometimes I meet with an author who does all who he can to make the human shape more than divine. Thus is the spell dissolved, nor can it be wondered at if I throw the book from me in disgust.

Mrs. S. Green,
Romance Readers and Romance Writers: A Satirical Novel (1810)
1152.c.1

28 October

That Utimate Test

Nothing, of course, will ever take the place of the good old fashion of 'liking' a work of art or not liking it: the most improved criticism will not abolish that primitive, that ultimate test.

Henry James,
'The Art of Fiction', in *Partial Portraits* (1888)
10601.bbb.12

 29 October

Shine on

How the great poets do shine on ...! Into all the dark corners of the world. They have no night.

Willa Cather,
My Mortal Enemy (1926)
012640.b.112

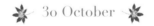 30 October

The Dunghill of the World

Flies sit at times on the sweetmeats that are exposed for sale in the shop of a confectioner; but as soon as the sweeper passes by with his basket of filth the flies leave the sweetmeats to settle on it. The honey bee never sits on filth but only on flowers. Worldly men are like flies. They may get a taste of the Divine Sweetness but their natural tendency towards dirt soon brings them back to the dunghill of the world.

Ramakrishna,
q. in Peter France, *Hermits: The Insights of Solitude* (1996)
YC.1996.b.5638

 31 October

Biological Chauffeurs and Repair Men

Every person has a skeleton of his own. To become better acquainted with it is a source of intellectual delight and satisfaction. [...] The wise owner of an automobile is curious to understand for himself the mechanism of his particular machine in order not to depend entirely upon a chauffeur or repair man. An equal amount of curiosity about the individual human organism, which one personifies, is not only pardonable, but also almost imperative if in an emergency one is not to resort helplessly to biological chauffeurs and repair men, otherwise known as doctors and surgeons.

Herbert Eugene Walter,
The Human Skeleton: An Interpretation (1918)

7422.de.14

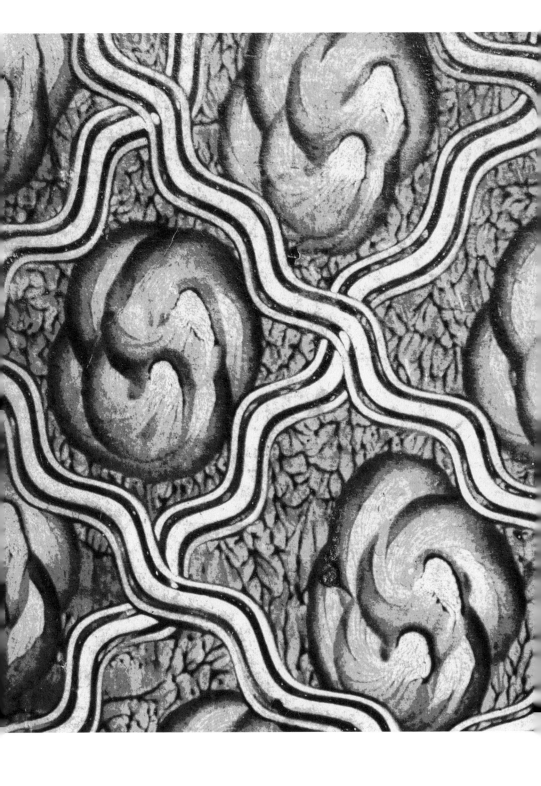

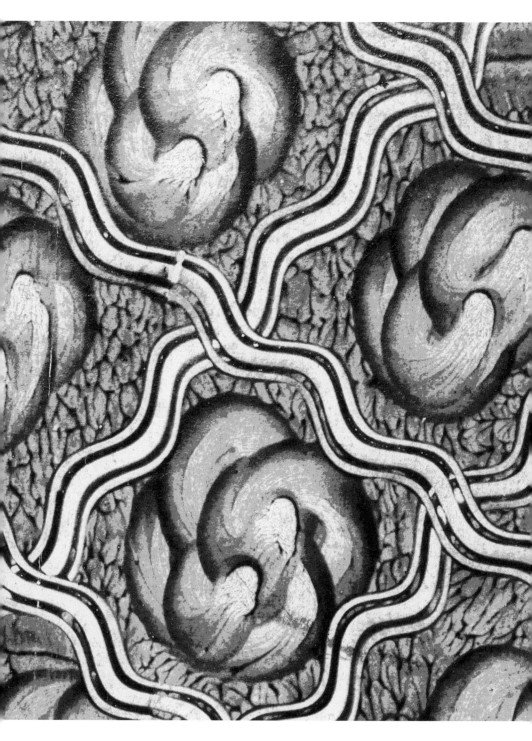

NOVEMBER

> ❧ 1 November ❧

Those Paper Prisons

DUCHESS: Who am I?

BOSOLA: Thou art a box of worm-seed, at best, but a salvatory of green mummy: – what's this flesh? a little crudded milk, fantastical puff-paste; our bodies are weaker than those paper prisons boys use to keep flies in; more contemptible, since ours is to preserve earth-worms.

John Webster, *The Duchess of Malfy* (1614; 1623 edn)
644.f.72

❧ 2 November ❦

What You Really Are

'The moment I met you I saw that you were quite unconscious of what you really are, what you really might be. There was so much about you that charmed me that I felt I must tell you something about yourself. I thought how tragic it would be if you were wasted. For there is such a little time that your youth will last, – such a little time.

'The common hill-flowers wither, but they blossom again. The laburnum will be as golden next June as it is now. In a month there will be purple stars on the clematis, and year after year the green night of its leaves will have its purple stars. But we never get back our youth. The pulse of joy that beats in us at twenty, becomes sluggish. Our limbs fail, our senses rot. We degenerate into hideous puppets, haunted by the memory of the passions of which we were too much afraid, and the exquisite temptations that we did not dare to yield to. Youth! Youth! There is absolutely nothing in the world but youth!'

Dorian Gray listened, open-eyed and wondering. The spray of lilac fell from his hand upon the gravel. A furry bee came and buzzed round it for a moment. Then it began to scramble all over the fretted purple of the tiny blossoms. He watched it with that strange interest in trivial things that we try to develop when things of high import make us afraid, or when we are stirred by some new emotion, for which we cannot find expression, or when some thought that terrifies us lays sudden siege to the brain and calls on us to yield. After a time it flew away. He saw it creeping into the stained trumpet of a Tyrian convolvulus. The flower seemed to quiver, and then swayed gently to and fro.

Oscar Wilde,
The Picture of Dorian Gray (1890; 1904 edn)
X.900/986

⟩ 3 November ⟨

An Affectionate Machine-Tickling Aphid?

Who shall say that man does see or hear? He is such a hive and swarm of parasites that it is doubtful whether his body is not more theirs than his, and whether he is anything but another kind of ant-heap after all. May not man himself become a sort of parasite upon the machines? An affectionate machine-tickling aphid?

Samuel Butler, *Erewhon* (1872)

12654.bb.3

❯ 4 November ❮

Do Not Hate Yourself

Do not hate yourself. Either spend the money without compunction, or, if you have compunction, don't spend it. A sinner should always, I think, sin gaily or not at all. I don't mean that you in this are a sinner; I only mean that as a general principle half-hearted sinners are contemptible. It is a poor creature who while he sins is sorry. If he must sin, let him at least do it with all his heart, and having done it waste no time in whimpers, but try to turn his back on it and his face towards the good. Please do not hate yourself. [...] It does no good and lowers your vitality. It is as bad as sorrow, which surely is very bad. I think nothing great was done by any one who wasted time peering about among his faults; but if ever you meet the pastor who prepared me for confirmation, don't tell him I said so.

'Elizabeth' [Elizabeth von Arnim, Lady Russell],
Fräulein Schmidt and Mr. Anstruther:
Being the Letters of an Independent Woman (1907)

012630.b.40

❯ 5 November ❮

Make No Secret of Low Spirits

Dear Lady Georgiana,

Nobody has suffered more from low spirits than I have done –
so I feel for you.

1st. Live as well as you dare.
2nd. Go into the shower-bath with a small quantity of water at a
temperature low enough to give you a slight sensation of cold,
75° or 80°.
3rd. Amusing books.
4th. Short views of human life—not further than dinner or tea.
5th. Be as busy as you can.
6th. See as much as you can of those friends who respect and like you.
7th. And of those acquaintances who amuse you.
8th. Make no secret of low spirits to your friends, but talk of them freely –
they are always worse for dignified concealment.
9th. Attend to the effects tea and coffee produce upon you.
10th. Compare your lot with that of other people.
11th. Don't expect too much from human life – a sorry business at the best.
12th. Avoid poetry, dramatic representations (except comedy), music, serious
novels, melancholy sentimental people, and every thing likely to excite feeling
or emotion not ending in active benevolence.
13th. Do good, and endeavour to please everybody of every degree.
14th. Be as much as you can in the open air without fatigue.
15th. Make the room where you commonly sit, gay and pleasant.
16th. Struggle by little and little against idleness.
17th. Don't be too severe upon yourself, or underrate yourself, but do
yourself justice.
18th. Keep good blazing fires.
19th. Be firm and constant in the exercise of rational religion.
20th. Believe me, dear Georgiana, your devoted servant, Sydney Smith

Sydney Smith, 16 February 1820,
in *Selected Writings of Sydney Smith* (1956)

W63/0100

❯ 6 November ❮

You Will Not Forget It

In watching the infancy of my own children, I made another discovery – it is well known to mothers, to nurses, and also to philosophers – that the tears and lamentations of infants during the year or so when they have no other language of complaint run through a gamut that is as inexhaustible as the Cremona of Paganini. An ear but moderately learned in that language cannot be deceived as to the rate and modulus of the suffering which it indicates. A fretful or peevish cry cannot by any efforts make itself impassioned. The cry of impatience, of hunger, of irritation, of reproach, of alarm, are all different – different as a chorus of Beethoven from a chorus of Mozart. But if ever you saw an infant suffering for an hour, as sometimes the healthiest does, under some attack of the stomach, which has the tiger-grasp of the Oriental cholera, then you will hear moans that address to their mothers an anguish of supplication for aid such as might storm the heart of Moloch. Once hearing it, you will not forget it.

Thomas De Quincey, *Suspiria de Profundis* [1845–],
in *De Quincey's Works*, vol.16 (1871)
X12/2444

⤜ 7 November ⤛

The Sight of a Frog

Your Child shrieks and runs away at the Sight of a Frog, let another catch it and lay it down at a good Distance from him: at first accustom him to look upon it; when he can do that, then to come nearer to it and see it leap without Emotion; then to touch it lightly, when it is held fast in another's Hand; and so on, until he can come to handle it as confidently as a Butterfly or Sparrow. By the same way any other vain Terrors may be removed; if care be taken, that you go not too fast, and push not the Child on to a new Degree of Assurance, till he be thoroughly confirm'd in the former. And thus the young Soldier is to be train'd on to the Warfare of Life; wherein Care is to be taken, that more things be not represented as dangerous than really are so; and then, that whatever you observe him to be more frighted at than he should, you be sure to toll him on to by insensible Degrees, till he at last quitting his Fears, masters the Difficulty, and comes off with Applause.

John Locke,
An Essay Concerning Human Understanding (1690)
4454.c.20

> 8 November <

A Use for the Head of a Rat

Take the Head of a Rat or Mouse, pull the Skin from it, and carry the Head where the Mice and Rats come, and they wil be immediately gone from thence, Running altogether as if they were bewitched, and come no more.

The Compleat English and French Vermin-killer (c.1705)

969.a.47

> 9 November <

Of the Matter of Wherewith

God would be much honoured

1 By finding out the use of the fixed stars.
2 Of the matter of wherewith the Globe of the Earth is fill'd.
3 The use of most animals, vegetables, & mineralls.
4 The origins of man & animalls.
5 Of animals eating one another.
6 Of the pain& evils which animalls suffer.
7 Of generation by the way of male & female.
8 Of the different ages & gestation of animalls.
9 Of germination in animalls, vegeatables &c.

William Petty, *The Petty Papers:*
Some Unpublished Writings of William Petty,
ed. Marquis of Landsowne (1927)

W18/2644

> ❧ 10 November ❧

3,155,760,000

Dr Hooke, the famous English mathematician and philosopher, made a calculation of the number of separate ideas the mind is capable of entertaining, which he estimated as 3,155,760,000. – Haler, *Elementa Physiologiae*, vol.v, p. 547.

Oliver Wendell Holmes,
Pages from an Old Volume of Life:
A Collection of Essays, 1857–1881 (1883)

> 11 November ‹

Sweet Accord

Throughout the world, if it were sought,
Fair words enough a man shall find.
They be good cheap; they cost right naught;
Their substance is but only wind.
But well to say and so to mean –
That sweet accord is seldom seen.

Thomas Wyatt, 'Of Dissembling Words',
q. in *Sir Thomas Wyatt and His Poems,*
William Edward Simonds (1889)

10855.aaa.29

> 12 November ‹

Ferned Grot

A garden is a lovesome thing, God wot!
Rose plot,
Fringed pool,
Ferned grot –
The veriest school
Of peace; and yet the fool
Contends that God is not –
Not God! in gardens! when the eve is cool?
Nay, but I have a sign;
'Tis very sure God walks in mine.

Thomas Edward Brown, 'My Garden',
in *The Collected Poems of T. E. Brown* (1909)

11607.f.18

❥ 13 November ❧

Your Niche in Creation

You're neither unnatural, nor abominable, nor mad; you're as much a part of what people call nature as anyone else; only you're unexplained as yet – you've not got your niche in creation.

Radclyffe Hall, *The Well of Loneliness* (1928)

Cup.802.c.11

❥ 14 November ❧

The Most Merciful Thing in the World

The most merciful thing in the world, I think, is the inability of the human mind to correlate all its contents.

H. P. Lovecraft, 'The Call of Cthulhu' (1928), in *The Outsider and Others* (1939)

X.981/2620

⟩ 15 November ⟨

A Poor Stick, a Mere Stick

Among other comparative injuries which we are accustomed to do to the characters of things animate and inanimate, in order to gratify our human vanity, – such as calling a rascal a dog (which is a great compliment), and saying that a tyrant makes a beast of himself (which it would be a very good thing, and a lift in the world, if he could), is a habit, in which some persons indulge themselves, of calling insipid things and persons 'sticks.' Such and such a one is said to write a stick; and such another is himself called a stick; – a poor stick, a mere stick, a stick of a fellow.

We protest against this injustice to those genteel, jaunty, useful, and once flourishing sons of a good old stock. Take, for instance, a common cherry-stick, which is one of the favourite sort. In the first place, it is a very pleasant substance to look at, the grain running round it in glossy and shadowy rings. Then it is of primeval antiquity, handed down from scion to scion through the most flourishing of genealogical trees. In the third place, it is of Easter origin; of a stock, which is possible may have furnished Haroun al Raschid with a djereed, or Mohammed with a camel-stick, or Xenophon in his famous retreat with fences, or Xerxes with tent-pins, or Alexander with a javelin, or Sardanapalus with tarts, or Solomon with a simile for his mistresses' lips, or Jacob with a crook, or Methusaleh with shadow, or Zoraster with mathematical instruments, or the builders of Babel with scaffolding. Lastly, how do you know but that you may have eaten cherries off this very stick? for it was once alive with sap, and rustling with foliage, and powdered with blossoms, and red and laughing with fruit. Where the leathern tassel now hangs, may have hanged a bunch of berries; and instead of the brass ferrule poking in the mud, the tip was growing into the air with its youngest green.

Leigh Hunt, 'Of Sticks',
Essays by Leigh Hunt, ed. Edmund Oliver (1890)
X17/5295

> 16 November <

New Opportunities (And New Traps)

From the moment that humans began etching grooves into ancient wizard bones to mark the cycles of the moon, the process of encoding thought and experience into a vehicle of expression has influenced the changing nature of self. Information technology tweaks our perceptions, communicates our picture of the world to one another, and constructs remarkable and sometimes insidious forms of control over the cultural stories that shape our senses of the world. The moment we invent a significant device for communication – talking drums, papyrus scrolls, printed books, crystal sets, computers, pagers – we partially reconstruct the self and its world, creating new opportunities (and new traps) for thought, perception and social experience.

Erik Davis, *Techgnosis: Myth, Magic and Mysticism in the Age of Information* (1998)

YC.1999.a.2217

➤ 17 November ❮

There's a Boat Floating On Top of It

Scientific discovery is like the fitting together of the pieces of a great jig-saw puzzle; a revolution of science does not mean that the pieces already arranged and interlocked have to be dispersed; it means that in fitting on fresh pieces we have had to revise our impression of what the puzzle-picture is going to be like. One day you ask the scientist how he is getting on; he replies, 'Finely. I have very nearly finished this piece of blue sky.' Another day you ask how the sky is progressing and are told, 'I have added a lot more, but it was sea, not sky; there's a boat floating on the top of it.'

Sir Arthur Eddington,
The Nature of the Physical World (1928)
4175.260000 1927

➤ 18 November ❮

That Involuntary, Palpitating Life

She opened her curtains, and looked out towards the bit of road that lay in view, [...] Far off in the bending sky was the pearly light; and she felt the largeness of the world and the manifold wakings of men to labour and endurance. She was a part of that involuntary, palpitating life, and could neither look out on it from her luxurious shelter as a mere spectator, nor hide her eyes in selfish complaining.

George Eliot,
Middlemarch: A study of provincial life (1871)
Cup.404.b.11

❯ 19 November ❮

The Faces of the Sky

But for the faces of the Sky, they are so many, that many of them want proper names; and therefore it will be convenient to agree upon some determinate ones, by which the most usual may be in brief exprest. As let *Cleer* signifie a very cleer Sky with¬out any Clouds or Exhalations: *Checker'd* a cleer Sky, with many great white round Clouds, such as are very usual in Summer. *Hazy*, a Sky that looks whitish, by reason of the thickness of the higher parts of the Air, by some Exhalation not formed into Clouds. *Thick*, a Sky more whitened by a greater company of Vapours: these do usually make the *Luminaries* look bearded or hairy, and are oftentimes the cause of the appearance of Rings and Haloes about the *Sun* as well as the *Moon*. *Overcast*, when the Vapours so whiten and thicken the Air, that the *Sun* cannot break through; and of this there are very many degrees, which may be exprest by a *little, much, more, very much overcast*, &c. Let *Hairy* signifie a Sky that hath many small, thin and high Exhalations, which resemble locks of hair, or flakes of Hemp or Flax: whose varieties may be exprest by *straight* or *curv'd*, &c. according to the resemblance they bear. Let *Water'd* signifie a Sky that has many high thin and small Clouds, looking almost like water'd Tabby, called in some places a Mackeril Sky. Let a Sky be called *Waved*, when those Clouds appear much bigger and lower, but much after the same manner. *Cloudy*, when the Sky has many thick dark Clouds. *Lowring*, when the Sky is not very much overcast, but hath also underneath many thick dark Clouds which threaten rain. The signification of *gloomy, foggy, misty, sleeting, driving, rainy*, snowy, reaches or racks *variable*, &c. are well known, they being very commonly used. There may be also several faces of the Sky compounded of two or more of these, which may be intelligibly enough exprest by two or more of these names.

Robert Hooke, 'For the better Making a History of the Weather', in *The History of the Royal Society, For the Improving of Natural Knowledge*, Thomas Sprat (1667)

740.c.17

❧ 20 November ❦

Its Equal Ray

The sun, – the bright sun, that brings back, not light alone, but new life, and hope, and freshness to man – burst upon the crowded city in clear and radiant glory. Through costly-coloured glass and paper-mended window, through cathedral dome and rotten crevice, it shed its equal ray.

Charles Dickens, *Oliver Twist* (1839)

N.1532

❥ 21 November ❦

Honey Upon Sugar

I am constitutionally susceptible of noises. A carpenter's hammer, in a warm summer noon, will fret me into more than midsummer madness. But those unconnected, unset sounds are nothing to the measured malice of music. [...] I have sat through an Italian Opera, till, for sheer pain, and inexplicable anguish, I have rushed out into the noisiest place of the crowded streets, to solace myself with sounds, which I was not obliged to follow, and get rid of the distracting torment of endless, fruitless, barren attention! I take refuge in the unpretending assemblage of honest, common-life sounds; – and the purgatory of the Enraged Musician becomes my paradise. [...] Above all, those insufferable concertos, and pieces of music, as they are called, do plague and embitter my apprehension. – Words are something; but to be exposed to an endless battery of mere sounds; to be long a dying, to lie stretched upon a rack of roses; to keep up languor by unintermitted effort; to pile honey upon sugar, and sugar upon honey, to an interminable tedious sweetness; to fill up sound with feeling, and strain ideas to keep pace with it; to gaze on empty frames, and be forced to make the pictures for yourself; to a read a book, all stops, and be obliged to supply the verbal matter; to invent extempore tragedies to answer the vague gestures of an inexplicable rambling mime – these are faint shadows of what I have undergone from a series of the ablest-executed pieces of this empty instrumental music.

Charles Lamb, *Elia, Essays, Etc.* (1823)

Ashley1020

> 22 November <

Bore

He supposed that, except musicians, every one thought
Beethoven a bore, as every one except mathematicians
thought mathematics a bore.

Henry Adams,
The Education of Henry Adams (1907; 1918 edn)
W45308

> 23 November <

Simple Pleasure / Simple Pains

II. The several simple pleasures of which human nature is susceptible, seem to be as follows:
1. The pleasures of sense.
2. The pleasures of wealth.
3. The pleasures of skill.
4. The pleasures of amity.
5. The pleasures of a good name.
6. The pleasures of power.
7. The pleasures of piety.
8. The pleasures of benevolence.
9. The pleasures of malevolence.
10. The pleasures of memory.
11. The pleasures of imagination.
12. The pleasures of expectation.
13. The pleasures dependent on association.
14. The pleasures of relief.

III. The several simple pains seem to be as follows:
1. The pains of privation.
2. The pains of the senses.
3. The pains of awkwardness.
4. The pains of enmity.
5. The pains of an ill name.
6. The pains of piety.
7. The pains of benevolence.
8. The pains of malevolence.
9. The pains of the memory.
10. The pains of the imagination.
11. The pains of expectation
12. The pains dependent on association.

Jeremy Bentham,
An Introduction to the Principles of Morals and Legislation (1789)
C.61.e.4

⟩ 24 November ⟨

Mysterium Tremendum

Let us consider the deepest and most fundamental element in all strong and sincerely felt religious emotion. Faith unto Salvation, Trust, Love – all these are there. But over and above these is an element which may also on occasion, quite apart from them, profoundly affect us and occupy the mind with a well nigh bewildering strength. Let us follow it up with every effort of sympathy and imaginative intuition wherever it is to be found, in the lives of those around us, in sudden, strong ebullitions of personal piety and the frames of mind such ebullitions evince, in the fixed and ordered solemnities of rites and liturgies, and again in the atmosphere that clings to old religious monuments and buildings, to temples and to churches. If we do so we shall find we are dealing with something for which there is only one appropriate expression, *mysterium tremendum*. The feeling of it may at times come sweeping like a gentle tide, pervading the mind with a tranquil mood of deepest worship. It may pass over into a more set and lasting attitude of the soul, continuing, as it were, thrillingly vibrant and resonant, until at last it dies away and the soul resumes its 'profane', non-religious mood of everyday experience. It may burst in sudden eruption up from the depths of the soul with spasms and convulsions, or lead to the strangest excitements, to intoxicated frenzy, to transport, and to ecstasy. It has its wild and demonic forms and can sink to an almost grisly horror and shuddering. It has its crude, barbaric antecedents and early manifestations, and again it may be developed into something beautiful and pure and glorious. It may become the hushed, trembling and speechless humility of the creature in the presence of – whom or what? In the presence of that which is a *Mystery* inexpressible and above all creatures.

Rudolf Otto, *The Idea of the Holy: An Inquiry into the Non-Rational Factor in the Idea of the Divine and its Relation to the Rational*, trans. John W. Harvey (1923)

03558.f.34

❯ 25 November ❮

The Pleasure of Travel

The same things every day slowly kill us off. To crave anew, the pleasure of travel helps us to do this. It not merely freshens up the expectation before the journey starts, but does this in the midst of the enjoyment of seeing. Wishes which nothing can be done about any more, superannuated wishes which have become spinsterish, drop away. The stagnant element drops away, which may characterize not only everyday life that always remains the same, but also wishes carried around for all too long. Wishful dreams can after all have passed out of the time appropriate to them, in such a way that they can never again be fulfilled. Someone who wished for a Kodak in his youth and never got one will never again find the Kodak of his wishes, even if as a man he is in a position to buy the very best. Such things were not accorded to the desire at the time or in the circumstances when they would have given the most extreme pleasure. The hunger for them has gone grey, in fact almost every goal can become tedious if it is launched towards for too long, too hopelessly or even in too habitual a way. Whereas new wares create new needs, and in particular new impressions.

Ernst Bloch, *The Principle of Hope*, vol.1 (1954)
trans. Neville Plaice, Stephen Plaice, Paul Knight (1995)

97/14558

⟩ 26 November ⟨

Rolling Stones Like Me

Carl paused. Alexandra pushed her hair back from her brow with a puzzled, thoughtful gesture. 'You see,' he went on calmly, 'measured by your standards here, I'm a failure. I couldn't buy even one of your cornfields. I've enjoyed a great many things, but I've got nothing to show for it all.'

'But you show for it yourself, Carl. I'd rather have had your freedom than my land.'

Carl shook his head mournfully. 'Freedom so often means that one isn't needed anywhere. Here you are an individual, you have a background of your own, you would be missed. But off there in the cities there are thousands of rolling stones like me. We are all alike; we have no ties, we know nobody, we own nothing. When one of us dies, they scarcely know where to bury him. Our landlady and the delicatessen man are our mourners, and we leave nothing behind us but a frock-coat and a fiddle, or an easel, or a typewriter, or whatever tool we got our living by. All we have ever managed to do is to pay our rent, the exorbitant rent that one has to pay for a few square feet of space near the heart of things. We have no house, no place, no people of our own. We live in the streets, in the parks, in the theatres. We sit in restaurants and concert halls and look about at the hundreds of our own kind and shudder.'

Alexandra was silent. She sat looking at the silver spot the moon made on the surface of the pond down in the pasture. He knew that she understood what he meant. At last she said slowly, 'And yet I would rather have Emil grow up like that than like his two brothers. We pay a high rent, too, though we pay differently. We grow hard and heavy here. We don't move lightly and easily as you do, and our minds get stiff. If the world were no wider than my cornfields, if there were not something beside this, I wouldn't feel that it was much worth while to work.'

Willa Cather, *O Pioneers!* (1913)

012704.cc.43

> ❥ 27 November ❦

An Old Abode

Rambling I looked for an old abode
Where, years back, one had lived I knew;
Its site a dwelling duly showed,
But it was new.
I went where, not so long ago,
The sod had riven two breasts asunder;
Daisies throve gaily there, as though
No grave were under.
I walked along a terrace where
Loud children gambolled in the sun;
The figure that had once sat there
Was missed by none.
Life laughed and moved on unsubdued,
I saw that Old succumbed to Young:
'Twas well. My too regretful mood
Died on my tongue.

Thomas Hardy, 'Life Laughs Onwards',
from *Moments of Vision and Miscellaneous Verses* (1917)

011648.eee.54

> 28 November ‹

Where is He Now?

Still I would return some time or other to this enchanted spot; but I would return to it alone. What other self could I find to share that influx of thoughts, of regret, and delight, the fragments of which I could hardly conjure up to myself, so much have they been broken and defaced. I could stand on some tall rock, and overlook the precipice of years that separates me from what I then was. I was at that time going shortly to visit the poet whom I have above named. Where is he now? Not only I myself have changed; the world, which was then new to me, has become old and incorrigible. Yet will I turn to thee in thought, O sylvan Dee, in joy, in youth and gladness as thou then wert; and thou shalt always be to me the river of Paradise, where I will drink of the waters of life freely!

There is hardly anything that shows the shortsightedness or capriciousness of the imagination more than travelling does. With change of place we change our ideas; nay, our opinions and feelings. We can by an effort indeed transport ourselves to old and long-forgotten scenes, and then the picture of the mind revives again; but we forget those that we have just left. It seems that we can think but of one place at a time. The canvas of the fancy is but of a certain extent, and if we paint one set of objects upon it, they immediately efface every other. We cannot enlarge our conceptions, we only shift our point of view. The landscape bares its bosom to the enraptured eye, we take our fill of it, and seem as if we could form no other image of beauty or grandeur. We pass on, and think no more of it; the horizon that shuts it from our sight also blots it from our memory like a dream. In travelling through a wild barren country, I can form no idea of a woody and cultivated one. It appears to me that all the world must be barren, like what I see of it. In the country we forget the town, and in town we despise the country.

William Hazlitt, 'On Going a Journey', in *Table Talk*, vol.II (1822)

629.e.20-21

> ❯ 29 November ❮

This is Why We Are Hated

How they hate us, these foreigners, in Belgium as much as in France! What lies they tell of us; how gladly they would see us humiliated! Honest folks at home over their port-wine say, 'Ay, ay, and very good reason they have too. National vanity, sir, wounded – we have beaten them so often.' My dear sir, there is not a greater error in the world than this. They hate you because you are stupid, hard to please, and intolerably insolent and air-giving. I walked with an Englishman yesterday, who asked the way to a street of which he pronounced the name very badly to a little Flemish boy: the Flemish boy did not answer; and there was my Englishman quite in a rage, shrieking in the child's ear as if he must answer. He seemed to think that it was the duty of 'the snob,' as he called him, to obey the gentleman. This is why we are hated – for pride. In our free country a tradesman, a lackey, or a waiter will submit to almost any given insult from a gentleman: in these benighted lands one man is as good as another; and pray God it may soon be so with us! Of all European people, which is the nation that has the most haughtiness, the strongest prejudices, the greatest reserve, the greatest dulness? I say an Englishman of the genteel classes. An honest groom jokes and hobs-and-nobs and makes his way with the kitchen-maids, for there is good social nature in the man; his master dare not unbend. Look at him, how he scowls at you on your entering an inn-room; think how you scowl yourself to meet his scowl. To-day, as we were walking and staring about the place, a worthy old gentleman in a carriage, seeing a pair of strangers, took off his hat and bowed very gravely with his old powdered head out of the window: I am sorry to say that our first impulse was to burst out laughing – it seemed so supremely ridiculous that a stranger should notice and welcome another.

W. M. Thackeray, *The Paris Sketch Book
and Little Travels and Road-Side Sketches* (1879)

W 52/4967

❯ 30 November ❮

England's in a Horrid Mess

England's in a horrid mess, Mac o' my heart. We're all running after the moon. Some of us want to get rich by the unaided effort of others; others want to have their rights – only they don't know what they are, but they intend to have 'em. Others insist that the panacea for every evil is that the government should do it, and still more that the government should pay for it, as though Lloyd George had found a gold mine in the garden of No. 10 Downing St., and had only to put down his hand to supply us with our pensions, indemnities, two shillings a week rise in wages, cheap coal, electric massage, twopence a case divorce and railway transport. And at Oxford and other places where they still cherish ideas of Utopia, we weep because we can't make archangels out of men all in a hurry, forgetting it's taken a good many thousands of years to make a man out of a monkey, and when we think now and then we see his wings sprouting, we weep to find that the only superfluous excrescence on his person is a remnant of his monkey's tail!

Winifred Holtby, letter to Jean McWilliam (Rosalind),
26 September 1920, in *Letters to a Friend*,
eds Alice Holtby and Jean McWilliam (1937)

010921.f.1

DECEMBER

❧ 1 December ☙

A Comfortable Time-Lag

In England we have come to rely upon a comfortable time-lag of fifty years or a century intervening between the perception that something ought to be done and a serious attempt to do it.

H. G. Wells,
The Work, Wealth and Happiness of Mankind (1932)
8275.pp.21

2 December

When a Whole Nation is Smitten

Alas, my Friends, credulous incredulity is a strange matter. But when a whole Nation is smitten with Suspicion, and sees a dramatic miracle in the very operation of the gastric juices, what help is there? Such Nation is already a mere hypochondriac bundle of diseases; as good as changed into glass; atrabiliar, decadent; and will suffer crises. Is not Suspicion itself the one thing to be suspected, as Montaigne feared only fear?

Thomas Carlyle, *The French Revolution: A History* (1837)

W3/6436

3 December

England

Heaven be blessed, England is only a spot of grease on the soup just now.

D. H. Lawrence, *The Selected Letters of D. H. Lawrence,*
ed. James T. Boulton (1997)

YC.1997.b.1581

4 December

A Tide that Ebbs and Flows

[9 April 1905] [KONIA, Syria]

What a country this is! I fear I shall spend the rest of my life travelling in it. Race after race, one on top of the other, the whole land strewn with the mighty relics of them. We in Europe are accustomed to think that civilization is an advancing flood that has gone steadily forward since the beginning of time. I believe we are wrong. It is a tide that ebbs and flows, reaches a high water mark and turns back again.

Gertrude Bell, letter to Florence Lascelles,
in *The Letters of Gertrude Bell*, vol.1 (1927)
10922.ff.10

5 December

Commercial Crises

I have been repeatedly told by men who have good opportunity of hearing current opinions, that they who theorise about the relations of sun-spots, rainfall, famines, and commercial crises are supposed to be jesting, or at the best romancing. I am, of course, responsible only for a small part of what has been put forth on this subject, but so far as I am concerned in the matter, I beg leave to affirm that I never was more in earnest, and that after some further careful inquiry, I am perfectly convinced that these decennial crises do depend upon meteorological variations of like period, which again depend, in all probability, upon cosmic variations of which we have evidence in the frequency of sun-spots, auroras, and magnetic perturbations.

W. Stanley Jevons, *Investigations in Currency and Finance*,
ed. H. S. Foxwell (1884)
T 8407

❧ 6 December ❧

Consider What Nation It is Whereof Ye Are

Lords and Commons of England! consider what nation it is whereof ye are, and whereof ye are the governors: a nation not slow and dull, but of a quick, ingenious and piercing spirit, acute to invent, subtle and sinewy to discourse, not beneath the reach of any point the highest that human capacity can soar to. [...] A little generous prudence, a little forbearance of one another, and some grain of charity might win all these diligences to join, and unite in one general and brotherly search after truth; could we but forgo this prelatical tradition of crowding free consciences and Christian liberties into canons and precepts of men. [...] Yet these are the men cried out against for schismatics and sectaries; as if, while the temple of the Lord was building, some cutting, some squaring the marble, others hewing the cedars, there should be a sort of irrational men who could not consider there must be many schisms and many dissections made in the quarry and in the timber, ere the house of God can be built. And when every stone is laid artfully together, it cannot be united into a continuity, it can but be contiguous in this world; neither can every piece of the building be of one form; nay rather the perfection consists in this, that, out of many moderate varieties and brotherly dissimilitudes that are not vastly disproportional, arises the goodly and the graceful symmetry that commends the whole pile and structure.

Let us therefore be more considerate builders, more wise in spiritual architecture, when great reformation is expected.

John Milton, *Areopagitica* (1644),
ed. with a commentary by Sir Richard C. Jebb (1918)

2322.bb.27

7 December

These Proud Islanders

There are two words in their language on which these people pride themselves, and they say cannot be translated. *Home* is the one, by which an Englishman means his house [...] The other word is *comfort*; it means all the enjoyments and privileges of home; and here I must confess that these proud islanders have reasons for their pride. In their social intercourse and their modes of life they have enjoyments which we never dream of.

Robert Southey, *Letters from England: By Don Manuel Alvarez Epriella, Translated from the Spanish*, vol.1 (1807)

1508/377

8 December

Dere's No Escapin' It

Inglan is a bitch
dere's no escapin' it
Inglan is a bitch
dere's no runnin' whey fram it

Linton Kwesi Johnson, *Inglan Is a Bitch* (1970)

X.950/2492

༄ 9 December ༄

You Will Play the Game

The defects of the Englishman's qualities are strange in practice, but obvious enough when we consider the root fact from which they spring. And that root fact is simply that the Englishman feels very deeply and reasons very little. It might be argued, superficially, that because he has done little to remedy the state of things on the Congo, that he is lacking in feeling. But, as a matter of fact, it is really because he is aware – subconsciously if you will – of the depth of his capacity to feel, that the Englishman takes refuge in his particular official optimism. He hides from himself the fact that there are in the world greed, poverty, hunger, lust or evil passions, simply because he knows that if he comes to think of them at all they will move him beyond bearing. He prefers, therefore, to say – and to hypnotize himself into believing that the world is a very good – an all-good – place. He would prefer to believe that such people as the officials of the Congo Free State do not really exist in the modern world. People, he will say, do not do such things. [...] It is true that in repressing its emotions this people, so adventurous and so restless, has discovered the secret of living. For not the railway stations alone, these scenes of so many tragedies of meeting and parting, but every street and every office would be uninhabitable to a people could they see the tragedies that underlie life and voice the full of their emotions. Therefore, this people which has so high a mission in the world has invented a saving phrase which, upon all occasions, unuttered and perhaps unthought, dominates the situation. For, if in England we seldom think it and more seldom say it, we nevertheless feel very intimately as a set rule of conduct, whenever we meet a man, whenever we talk with a woman: 'You will play the game.'

Ford Madox Ford, *The Spirit of the People* (1907)

X25/1774

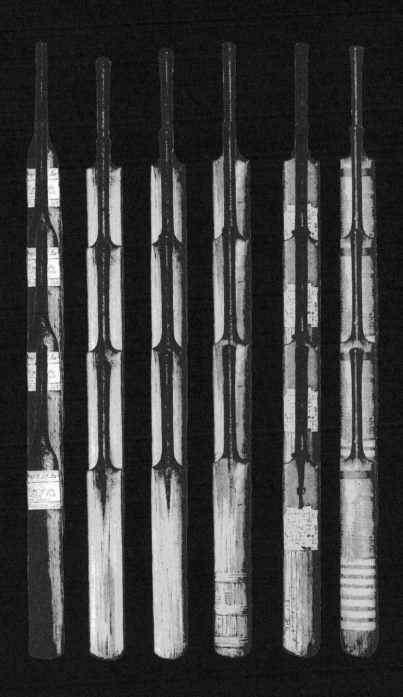

10 December

Sever That Cord

In any case, the purpose is not really to indict the past, but to summon it to the attention of a suicidal, anachronistic present. To say to that mutant present: you are a child of those centuries of lies, distortion and opportunism in high places, even among the holy of holies of intellectual objectivity. But the world is growing up, while you wilfully remain a child, a stubborn, self-destructive child, with certain destructive powers, but a child nevertheless. And to say to the world, to call attention to its own historic passage of lies – as yet unabandoned by some – which sustains the evil precocity of this child. Wherein then lies the surprise that we, the victims of that intellectual dishonesty of others, demand from that world that is finally coming to itself, a measure of expiation? Demand that it rescues itself, by concrete acts, from the stigma of being the wilful parent of a monstrosity, especially as that monstrous child still draws material nourishment, breath, and human recognition from the strengths and devises of that world, with an umbilical cord which stretches across oceans, even across the cosmos via so-called programmes of technological co-operation. We are saying very simply but urgently: Sever that cord. By any name, be it Total Sanction, Boycott, Disinvestment, or whatever, sever this umbilical cord and leave this monster of a birth to atrophy and die or to rebuild itself on long-denied humane foundations. Let it collapse, shorn of its external sustenance, let it collapse of its own social disequilibrium, its economic lopsidedness, its war of attrition on its most productive labour. Let it wither like an aborted foetus of the human family if it persists in smothering the minds and sinews which constitute its authentic being.

Wole Soyinka, 'This Past Must Address its Present',
Nobel Lecture (1986) in *Nobel lectures: 20 years of the
Nobel Prize for Literature lectures* (2007)

YC.2008.a.10804

11 December

Take a Natural Posture

Why shall History go on kneeling to the end of time? I am for having her rise up off her knees and take a natural posture: not to be for ever shuffling backwards out of doors in the presence of the sovereign.

W. M. Thackeray, *The History of Henry Esmond* (1852)

W62/8489

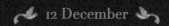 12 December

That Is Government

To be GOVERNED is to be watched, inspected, spied upon, directed, law-driven, numbered, regulated, enrolled, indoctrinated, preached at, controlled, checked, estimated, censured, commanded, by creatures who have neither the right nor the wisdom nor the virtue to do so. To be GOVERNED is to be at every operation, at every transaction, noted, registered, counted, taxed, stamped, measured, numbered, assessed, licensed, authorized, admonished, prevented, forbidden, reformed, corrected, punished. It is, under pretext of public utility, and in the name of the general interest, to be placed under contribution, drilled, fleeced, exploited, monopolized, extorted from, squeezed, hoaxed, robbed; then, at the slightest resistance, the first word of complaint, to be repressed, fined, vilified, harassed, hunted down, abused, clubbed, disarmed, bound, choked, imprisoned, judged, condemned, shot, deported, sacrificed, sold, betrayed; and to crown all, mocked, ridiculed, derided, outraged, dishonoured. That is government; that is its justice; that is its morality.

Pierre Joseph Proudhon,
*General Idea of the Revolution
in the Nineteenth Century* (1851),
trans. John Beverly Robinson (1923)

08007.de.30

13 December

The Final Period of Our State Approaches

The truth is, our symptoms are so bad that, notwithstanding all the care and vigilance of the legislature, it is to be feared that the final period of our state approaches. Strong constitutions, whether politic or natural, do not feel light disorders. But when they are sensibly affected, the distemper is for the most part violent, and of all ill prognostic. Free governments like our own were planted by the Goths in most parts of Europe; and, though we all know what they are come to, yet we seem rather disposed to follow their example than to profit by it.

God grant the time be not near when men shall say: 'This island was once inhabited by a religious, brave, sincere people, of plain uncorrupt manners, respecting inbred wealth rather than titles and appearances, asserters of liberty, lovers of their country, jealous of their own rights, and unwilling to infringe the rights of others; improvers of learning and useful arts, enemies to luxury, tender of other men's lives and prodigal of their own; inferior in nothing to the old Greeks or Romans, and superior to each of those people in the perfections of the other. Such were our ancestors during their rise and greatness; but they degenerated, grew servile flatterers of men in power, adopted Epicurean notions, became venal, corrupt, injurious, which drew upon them the hatred of God and man, and occasioned their final ruin.'

George Berkeley, *An Essay Towards*
Preventing the Ruine of Great Britain (1721)

T.1108.(25.)

14 December

You Will Take Up New Causes

Anyone can become part of the critical mass that offers us a chance of improving the world before it is too late. You can rethink your goals and question what you are doing with your life. If your present way of living does not stand up against an impartial standard of value, then you can change it. That might mean quitting your job, selling your house, and going to work for a voluntary organization in India. More often, the commitment to a more ethical way of living will be the first step of a gradual but far-reaching evolution in your lifestyle and in your thinking about your place in the world. You will take up new causes and find your goals shifting. If you get involved in your work, money and status will become less important. From your new perspective, the world will look different. One thing is certain: you will find plenty of worthwhile things to do. You will not be bored or lack fulfilment in your life. Most important of all, you will know that you have not lived and died for nothing, because you will have become part of the great tradition of those who have responded to the amount of pain and suffering in the universe by trying to make the world a better place.

Peter Singer, *How Are We to Live?*
Ethics in an age of self-interest (1994)

YK.1996.a.7182

The Central Capabilities

1. Life. Being able to live to the end of a human life of normal length; not dying prematurely, or before one's life is so reduced as to be not worth living.

2. Bodily Health. Being able to have good health, including reproductive health; to be adequately nourished; to have adequate shelter.

3. Bodily Integrity. Being able to move freely from place to place; to be secure against violent assault, including sexual assault and domestic violence; having opportunities for sexual satisfaction and for choice in matters of reproduction.

4. Senses, Imagination, and Thought. Being able to use the senses, to imagine, think, and reason – and to do these things in a 'truly human' way, a way informed and cultivated by an adequate education, including, but by no means limited to, literacy and basic mathematical and scientific training. Being able to use imagination and thought in connection with experiencing and producing works and events of one's own choice, religious, literary, musical, and so forth. Being able to use one's mind in ways protected by guarantees of freedom of expression with respect to both political and artistic speech, and freedom of religious exercise. Being able to have pleasurable experiences and to avoid non-beneficial pain.

5. Emotions. Being able to have attachments to things and people outside ourselves; to love those who love and care for us, to grieve at their absence; in general, to love, to grieve, to experience longing, gratitude, and justified anger. Not having one's emotional development blighted by fear and anxiety. (Supporting this capability means supporting forms of human association that can be shown to be crucial in their development.)

6. Practical Reason. Being able to form a conception of the good and to engage in critical reflection about the planning of one's life. (This entails protection for the liberty of conscience and religious observance.)

7. Affiliation.
A. Being able to live with and toward others, to recognize and show concern for other human beings, to engage in various forms of social interaction; to be able to imagine the situation of another. (Protecting this capability means protecting institutions that constitute and nourish such forms of affiliation, and also protecting the freedom of assembly and political speech.) **B.** Having the social bases of self-respect and non-humiliation; being able to be treated as a dignified being whose worth is equal to that of others. This entails provisions of non-discrimination on the basis of race, sex, sexual orientation, ethnicity, caste, religion, national origin.

8. Other Species. Being able to live with concern for and in relation to animals, plants, and the world of nature.

9. Play. Being able to laugh, to play, to enjoy recreational activities.

10. Control over one's Environment.
A. Political. Being able to participate effectively in political choices that govern one's life; having the right of political participation, protections of free speech and association.
B. Material. Being able to hold property (both land and movable goods), and having property rights on an equal basis with others; having the right to seek employment on an equal basis with others; having the freedom from unwarranted search and seizure. In work, being able to work as a human being, exercising practical reason and entering into meaningful relationships of mutual recognition with other workers.

Martha Nussbaum, 'Capabilities as fundamental entitlements:
Sen and social justice', in *Amartya Sen's Work and Ideas:*
A Gender Perspective, eds Bina Agarwal,
Jane Humphries & Ingrid Robeyns (2005)

mo5/.33293

16 December

It Is Curious

It surely may be considered curious as being the first attempt to publish the history of a people, from the lips of the people themselves – giving a literal description of their labour, their earnings, their trials, and their sufferings, in their own 'unvarnished' language; and to portray the condition of their homes and their families by personal observation of the places, and direct communion with the individuals.

It may be considered curious also as being the first commission of inquiry into the state of the people undertaken by a private individual, and the first 'blue book' ever published in twopenny numbers.

It is curious, moreover, as supplying information concerning a large body of persons, of whom the public had less knowledge than of the most distant tribes of the earth – the government population returns not even numbering them among the inhabitants of the kingdom; and as adducing facts so extraordinary, that the traveller in the undiscovered country of the poor must, like Bruce, until his stories are corroborated by after investigators, be content to lie under the imputation of telling such tales, as travellers are generally supposed to delight in.

Henry Mayhew,
London Labour and the London Poor (1861–62)

08275.bb.28

17 December

The Fundamental Obligations of Kinship

The idea that kinship is not purely an affair of birth, but may be acquired, has quite fallen out of our circle of ideas; but so, for that matter, has the primitive conception of kindred itself. To us kinship has no absolute value, but is measured by degrees, and means much or little, or nothing at all, according to its degree and other circumstances. In ancient times, on the contrary, the fundamental obligations of kinship had nothing to do with degrees of relationship, but rested with absolute and identical force on every member of the clan. To know that a man's life was sacred to me, and that every blood-feud that touched him involved me also, it was not necessary for me to count cousinship with him by reckoning up to our common ancestor; it was enough that we belonged to the same clan and bore the same clan-name.

W. Roberston Smith,
Lectures on the Religion of the Semites (1889)
4506.ee.3

18 December

Thought of the Second Degree

Philosophy is reflective. The philosophising mind never simply thinks about an object, it always, while thinking about any object, thinks also about its own thought about that object. Philosophy may thus be called thought of the second degree, thought about thought. For example, to discover the distance of the earth from the sun is a task for thought of the first degree, in this case for astronomy; to discover what it is exactly that we are doing when we discover the distance of the earth from the sun is a task for thought of the second degree, in this instance for logic or the theory of science.

R. G. Collingwood, *The Idea of History* (1946)

901 *749*

19 December

A Scar of Indelible Intolerance

But future facts had to be solved, which undoubtedly would be treated with more comparative reverence than heretofore, by him who suffered severely – yea, acutely – from the blow struck him on the eve of aspiration and achievement. Love, alas! when smitten with the sword of indifference, dieth soon, but once struck on the tunnelled cheek of secrecy with the hand of pity there leaves a scar of indelible intolerance, until wiped out for ever with the curative balsam of battled freedom.

Amanda McKittrick Ros, *Irene Iddesleigh* (1897)

012621.m.17

20 December

A Parcel of Big Words

It is not easy to write a familiar style. Many people mistake a familiar for a vulgar style, and suppose that to write without affectation is to write at random. On the contrary, there is nothing that requires more precision, and, if I may so say, purity of expression, than the style I am speaking of. It utterly rejects not only all unmeaning pomp, but all low, cant phrases, and loose, unconnected, slipshod allusions. It is not to take the first word that offers, but the best word in common use; it is not to throw words together in any combinations we please, but to follow and avail ourselves of the true idiom of the language. To write a genuine familiar or truly English style, is to write as any one would speak in common conversation who had a thorough command and choice of words, or who could discourse with ease, force, and perspicuity, setting aside all pedantic and oratorical flourishes . . . It is easy to affect a pompous style, to use a word twice as big as the thing you want to express: it is not so easy to pitch upon the very word that exactly fits it. [...] I hate anything that occupies more space than it is worth. I hate to see a load of band-boxes go along the street, and I hate to see a parcel of big words without anything in them.

William Hazlitt, 'On Familiar Style',
in *Table Talk*, vol.II (1822)

629.e.20-21

21 December

Very Nearly Akin to the Repulsive

In the Munich beer halls, when one student is heard laying down the law about something which he does not understand to a companion who cares not a rap on the subject, it is very generally taken for granted that the two are talking metaphysics. Indeed, metaphysics has a bad name everywhere. In itself, it suggests nothing very enticing, and even its nomenclature seems to bring with it a sort of ponderosity which is very nearly akin to the repulsive.

Edgar Evertson Saltus,
The Philosophy of Disenchantment (1885)
8468.bb.23

22 December

The Shreds and Clippings of the Rest

On the fifth day of November, 1718, which to the aera fixed on,
was as near nine kalendar months as any husband could in
reason have expected, – was I Tristram Shandy, Gentleman,
brought forth into this scurvy and disastrous world of ours. –
I wish I had been born in the Moon, or in any of the planets,
(except Jupiter or Saturn, because I never could bear cold
weather) for it could not well have fared worse with me in any
of them (though I will not answer for Venus) than it has in
this vile, dirty planet of ours, – which, o' my conscience, with
reverence be it spoken, I take to be made up of the shreds
and clippings of the rest; – not but the planet is well enough,
provided a man could be born in it to a great title or to a great
estate; or could any how contrive to be called up to public
charges, and employments of dignity or power; – but that is
not my case; – and therefore every man will speak of the fair
as his own market has gone in it; – for which cause I affirm it
over again to be one of the vilest worlds that ever was made;
– for I can truly say, that from the first hour I drew my breath
in it, to this, that I can now scarce draw it at all, for an asthma
I got in scating against the wind in Flanders; – I have been
the continual sport of what the world calls Fortune.

Laurence Sterne, *The Life and Opinions of
Tristram Shandy, Gentleman* (1759; 1926 edn)

or2634.n.53

23 December

They

They like being living. They are not interested in this thing. They are quickly being existing. They are interested in this thing. They have been existing. They are not interested in this thing. They are going on being living. They are not interested in this thing. They are deciding something. They are not interested in that thing. They are doing something, they are going to be doing something. They are interested in that thing. They are going to be doing some other thing. They are interested in that thing. They are quicker than others who are slower. They are not interested in that thing. They are slower than others who are quicker. They are not interested in that thing. They are quicker than others who are slower. That is astonishing but not to them. They are slower than others who are quicker. That is not astonishing and not to them. They are quicker and they are slower and certainly this is in all of them and certainly this is astonishing to some coming to understand this thing. They are certainly deciding something. They are not interested in this thing. They are interested in everything. They are expecting something. They are not certain that they will be expecting something. They are deciding something then. They are not interested in this thing in deciding something, in having been deciding something.

Gertrude Stein, 'Italians',
in *Geography and Plays* (1922)

011388.k.28

24 December

To Make Snow

To make Snow

Take a quart of thick Creame, and five or six whites of Eggs, a saucer of Sugar finely beaten and as much Rosewater, beat them all together and always as it riseth take it out with a spoon, then take a loaf of Bread, cut away the crust, set in a platter and a great Rosemary bush in the middest of it, then lay your Snow with a Spoon upon the Rosemary, and so serve it.

A Book of Fruit and Flowers (1653; facsimile edn 1984)

X.329/19213

25 December

This System

At last the dinner was all done, the cloth was cleared, the hearth swept, and the fire made up. The compound in the jug being tasted and considered perfect, apples and oranges were put upon the table, and a shovel-full of chestnuts on the fire. Then all the Cratchit family drew round the hearth, in what Bob Cratchit called a circle, meaning half a one; and at Bob Cratchit's elbow stood the family display of glass; two tumblers, and a custard-cup without a handle. These held the hot stuff from the jug, however, as well as golden goblets would have done; and Bob served it out with beaming looks, while the chestnuts on the fire sputtered and crackled noisily. Then Bob proposed: 'A Merry Christmas to us all, my dears. God bless us!'

Charles Dickens, *A Christmas Carol* (1843)

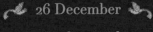 26 December

As Brisk as Wiskey

I

I am as brisk
As a bottle of Wisk-
Ey and as nimble
As a Milliner's thimble.

II

Oh, grant that like to Peter I
May like to Peter B,
And tell me, lovely Jesus, Y
Old Jonah went to C.

III

They weren fully glad of their gude hap
And tasten all the pleasaunces of joy

John Keats, fragments, in *The Poems of John Keats*,
ed. Miriam Allott (1970)

X.0909/105.(5.)

27 December

Deep Sad Thoughts

Shadows and scenes that have, for many hours,
Been my companions; I part from ye like friends –
Dear and familiar ones – with deep sad thoughts,
And hopes, almost misgivings!

Letitia Elizabeth Landon, 'The Farewell', from
Laman Blanchard, Life and Literary Remains of L.E.L. (1841)
C.116.bb.20

28 December

Now the Tale is Done

Thus grew the tale of Wonderland:
Thus slowly, one by one,
Its quaint events were hammered out –
And now the tale is done;
And home we steer, a merry crew,
Beneath the setting sun.

Lewis Carroll,
Alice's Adventures in Wonderland (1865)
C.59.g.32

❧ 29 December ❧

Almost to Heroic Pitch

The last volume was written in fourteen days. In this achievement Reardon rose almost to heroic pitch, for he had much to contend with beyond the mere labour of composition. Scarcely had he begun when a sharp attack of lumbago fell upon him; for two or three days it was torture to support himself at the desk, and he moved about like a cripple. Upon this ensued headaches, sore throat, general enfeeblement. And before the end of the fortnight it was necessary to think of raising another small sum of money; he took his watch to the pawnbroker's (you can imagine that it would not stand as security for much), and sold a few more books. All this notwithstanding, here was the novel at length finished. When he had written 'The End' he lay back, closed his eyes, and let time pass in blankness for a quarter of an hour.

It remained to determine the title. But his brain refused another effort; after a few minutes' feeble search he simply took the name of the chief female character, Margaret Home. That must do for the book. Already, with the penning of the last word, all its scenes, personages, dialogues had slipped away into oblivion; he knew and cared nothing more about them.

George Gissing, *New Grub Street* (1891)

W 6/4967

❧ 3o December ❧

Perhaps I am in Error

My instinct tells me that at the end of a novel or a story I must artfully concentrate for the reader an impression of the entire work, and therefore must casually mention something about those whom I have already presented. Perhaps I am in error.

Anton Chekhov, letter, 9 April 1888,
Letters on the Short Story, the Drama,
and other literary topics, ed. Louis S. Friedland (1924)

011840.bb.28

31 December

An Appreciable, If Inadequate, Something

Whether at, or towards, the conclusion of the present attempt the well-meaning adventurer is, to any considerable extent, in the traditional position of 'master' to himself as he was when he began it, I shall not pretend to say. That he is at least more conscious than ever of the audacity of the attempt itself, I can heartily asseverate. Yet the increased consciousness need not, I trust, be incompatible with a hope, if not a belief, that something at least has been attempted, even that an appreciable, if inadequate, something has been done. If I have not climbed the mountain, I think I may perhaps be allowed to have provided a convenient shop at its foot, where maps, and rope, and axes, and alpenstocks, and perhaps some provisions and stimulants for the journey, can be obtained a little more conveniently than they could be obtained before.

George Saintsbury,
A History of English Prose Rhythm (1912)
2308.g.10

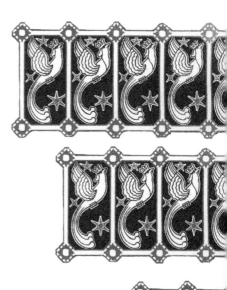

Acknowledgements

For previous acknowledgements see *The Truth About Babies* (2002), *Ring Road* (2004), *The Mobile Library: The Case of the Missing Books* (2006), *The Mobile Library: Mr Dixon Disappears* (2007), *The Mobile Library: The Delegates' Choice* (2008), *The Mobile Library: The Bad Book Affair* (2010), *Paper: An Elegy* (2012), *The Norfolk Mystery* (2013), *Death in Devon* (2015), *Westmorland Alone* (2016), *Essex Poison* (2017), *December Stories I* (2018), *The Sussex Murder* (2019), and *September 1, 1939: A Biography of a Poem* (2019). These stand, with exceptions. On this occasion I would like to thank my colleagues at Queen's University Belfast, the University of Warwick and Trinity College Dublin, and in particular Will Eaves, Stephen Kelly, Gail McConnell, Sarah Moss and Alex Murray, for generously sharing their knowledge and enthusiasms. Without Abigail Day and Jonny Davidson at the British Library this book would not have been possible.

List of Authors

Permissions and Copyright Acknowledgments

Acknowledgements are listed by the date for which the extract appears in this collection.

6 January *Changes* by Ama Ata Aidoo (1991), reproduced by permission of The Permissions Company, LLC; **13 January** © 1995 Barbara Kingsolver from *HIGH TIDE IN TUCSON: Essays From Now or Never*, reprinted by permission of The Frances Goldin Literary Agency; **14 January** *Beast and Man: The Roots of Human Nature* by Mary Midgely, published by Methuen, reproduced by permission of David Higham Associates Limited; **10 February** reprinted by permission of HarperCollins Publishers Ltd © Agatha Christie (1922); **27 February** *Another Time* by W. H. Auden, reproduced by permission of Curtis Brown, Ltd.; **20 March** *Letters from Iceland* by W. H. Auden and Louis MacNeice (extract by W. H. Auden), reproduced by permission of Curtis Brown, Ltd.; **28 March** reprinted by permission of The Society of Authors as the Literary Representative of the Estate of Rose Macaulay; **4 April** *At Swim-Two-Birds* by Flann O'Brien (Copyright © Flann O'Brien, 1939) Reproduced by permission of A.M. Heath & Co Ltd.; **9 April** *Clouds of Witness* by Dorothy L. Sayers, published by T. Fisher Unwin, reproduced by permission of David Higham Associates Limited; **13 April** *Form in Modern Poetry* by Herbert Read, published by Sheed & Ward, reproduced by permission of David Higham Associates Limited; **19 May** reprinted by permission of HarperCollins Publishers Ltd © Agatha Christie (1926); **20 June** reproduced by permissions of The Provost and Scholars of King's College, Cambridge and The Society of Authors as the E. M. Forster Estate; **29 June** *Understanding Media: The Extensions of Man* by Marshall McLuhan (1964), reproduced with permission courtesy of The MIT Press; **4 July** *I Remember* by Joe Brainard © The Estate of Joe Brainard, reproduced by permission of Library of America; **14 July** *Memento Mori* by Muriel Spark, published by Macmillan & Co, reproduced by permission of David Higham Associates Limited; **15 July** *The English Novelists: A Survey of the Novel by Twenty Contemporary Novelists*, ed. Derek Verschoyle, extract by Louis MacNeice, published by Chatto & Windus, reproduced by permission of David Higham Associates Limited; **16 July** © The Authors League Fund and St. Bride's Church, as joint literary executors of the Estate of Djuna Barnes; **26 July** © Candida Crewe, 2006, *Eating Myself*, Bloomsbury Publishing Plc; **2 August** *Sweet Memories: A Selection of Confectionery Delights* by Robert Opie (1999), reproduced by permission of Pavilion Books; **5 August** Stanton A. Glantz, John Slade, Lisa A. Bero, Peter Hanauer, Deborah E., *The Cigarette Papers*, 1996 © the authors, University of California Press; **9 August** *Travels with My Aunt* by Graham Greene, published by Heron Books, reproduced by permission of David Higham Associates Limited; **13 August** Rebecca Solnit, *Storming the Gates of Paradise*, 2007 © Rebecca Solnit, University of California Press; **25 August** *Autobiography / Bertrand Russell*, Bertrand Russell, Routledge, 2009; **29 August** © 2007 Foundation of the Works of C. G. Jung, Zürich; **31 August** 'An Interview with Robert Opie', in *The Cultures of Collecting* (1994), reproduced by permission of Reaktion Books; **26 September** *The English People* by George Orwell (Copyright © George Orwell, 1947) Reproduced by permission of A. M. Heath & Co Ltd.; **27 September** *In Defence of Vulgarity*, ed. Alan Heuser, extract by Louis MacNeice, published by Clarendon, reproduced by permission of David Higham Associates Limited; **3 October** *Traveller's Prelude* by Freya Stark, published by John Murray (1950), reproduced by permission of Hachette UK; **16 November** Text © Erik Davis, from *TechGnosis: Myth, Magic, and Mysticism in the Age of Information* (1998); **25 November** *The Principle of Hope* by Ernst Bloch, translation by Neville Plaice (1995), reproduced with permission courtesy of The MIT Press.

Reproduced by kind permission of the author or author's representative:
3 January © Slavoj Zizek; **29 January** © René Girard; **23 March** © Jerome McGann; **23 April** © Thomas Hine; **7 May** © Robert A. Erickson; **30 June** © Jean Baudrillard; **11 July** © Dr Elisabeth Kübler-Ross (www.EKRfoundation.org); **29 July** © David Greenberger; **21 August** © Germaine Greer; **22 October** © Eavan Boland; **24 October** © Sander Gilman; **8 December** © Linton Kwesi Johnson; **10 December** © Wole Soyinka; **14 December** © Peter Singer; **15 December** © Martha C. Nussbaum.